Drama for Reading and Performance

Collection One

D1091752

Perfection Learning® Corporation

Editorial Director Julie A. Schumacher
Senior Editor Gay Russell-Dempsey
Writer Sheri Reda
Design MaryAnn Lea
**Electronic
   Technology** Kay Ewald

Copyright 2000 by **Perfection Learning® Corporation**
   1000 North Second Avenue, P.O. Box 500
   Logan, Iowa 51546-0500
   Tel: 1-800-831-4190 • Fax: 1-712-644-2392

Printed in the United States of America
#78765 ISBN 0-7891-5205-3

Table of Contents

Drama for Reading and Performance

Table of Contents (cont)

The Arkansaw Bear

Plot Summary

In *The Arkansaw Bear,* Aurand Harris uses the metaphor of the circus to explore a child's confusion and fear in the face of death. Tish's grandfather is dying, and her mother and aunt would like to shield her from this sad reality. Tish runs off in an attempt to understand what is happening. What ensues is Tish's encounter with an interesting cast of characters. Like Tish's grandfather, Dancing Bear is also coming to the end of a long life. With the help of Mime, Dancing Bear determines to pass his skills and history on to Little Bear. When the Ringmaster finally comes to take Dancing Bear away, the bear has accomplished his task and is ready to go. Tish learns that death, while painful, must be accepted as a part of life.

The Play as Literature: Symbolism

Students might include some of the following symbols or words in their graphic organizers: Life: a tree with leaves/roots, flowers, a circle, the words *light* and *beginning.* Death: a skull and crossbones, a tree without leaves, dried leaves, a clock, the words *blackness* and *ending.*

You might also want to discuss the Ringmaster's role as a messenger of death and perhaps compare him to similar characters in literature, such as the Ghost of Christmas Future in *A Christmas Carol.* Talk about the meaning of the all-important Center Ring, as represented in the traditional circus as well as in the play. While death is often a touchy subject in our culture, and may be frightening to many students, most young people are very interested in the topic. You may want to explore the works of Elizabeth Kubler-Ross and her theory of the five stages of dying—most of which can be seen in this play—and share them with the students.

The Play as Theatre: Mime

Show an excerpt from a Charlie Chaplin or Buster Keaton silent film or a video of a performance by Marceau. Discuss with students how the actors communicate without words. Ask students which techniques they think are most effective and why. Have students brainstorm a list of different emotions. Then have them write each of these emotions on individual index cards. Have students—individually or in pairs—pick a card and act out the emotion for the class to identify.

Write the names of various sports or hobbies on the board (chess, swimming, mountain climbing—the more unusual the better!) Divide students into teams of three or four. Explain to students that they are spectators at these events. Have each group pick a different sport and pretend to watch it. Remind students to consider and establish the appropriate environment. Have students think about these questions: Does everyone react the same way? Is everyone always watching the event? How do the spectators interact?

WARM UP! Based on their descriptions of a treasured object, ask students to jot down a shorter description on an index card. Collect all the cards, and then pass them out to different students. Let each student take a few moments to read the description. Then remind them of Marcel Marceau and his ability to make his audience "see" an object. Ask for volunteers to mime the handling of this imaginary object and then have the class guess the item.

The Arkansaw Bear

Responding to the Play

1. Accept any reasonable well-supported response.
2. Symbols or words that might be added include: Life: growth, Little Bear dancing, a bright balloon, a tree, a footprint, a circle; Death: a cross, the unknown, the Ringmaster, a clock, a large book or ledger, sleep.
3. Dancing Bear drawings should indicate an understanding of the character and costuming directions.
4. Students might suggest that Star Bright would look "magical" in translucent, sparkling clothes. Perhaps a voice-enhancing mechanism or tape-recorded sound effects would offer an other-worldly effect. Suggested body movements might include a slow, yet generous movement of arms. Accept any well-thought-out, creative answers.
5. Program covers will vary and should reflect an understanding of the play.

For Further Discussion

1. What does Star Bright mean when he says " . . . the great circle of life. In every ending there is a new beginning"? (*Probably that life is a continuous cycle of birth and death; for every person who dies there is another being born.*)
2. When Tish dreams of a world where nobody would ever die, Star Bright replies, "Oh, no, no, no! Think what a mixed up world it would be!" Discuss with students how this could "mix up" the world.
3. What is the significance of the "living tree" standing alone onstage at the end of the play? (*Students may say that is a symbol of refuge, hope, growth, life, etc.*)

Creating and Performing

1. If students are having difficulty miming this section of the play, have them first narrate what they are trying to do. This will force them to sequence and correlate their movements to the narration.
2. If students cannot decide what position best illustrates a character's personality, have them brainstorm a list of descriptive words or actions for several characters.
3. Other ideas for a scene include Star Bright telling Tish about another person's wish he granted; Aunt Ellen and Tish having a more extensive discussion about death and the riddle of life.

Presenting the Play

For Reading

- Prepare students for the play's mature theme by discussing other pieces of literature you have read in class that deal with illness, dying, or death. Encourage students to describe how death was portrayed in other material they've read in class or on their own.

- To help students understand the Ringmaster's role as a symbol of death, ask a student to find the stage directions that tell how the Ringmaster dresses and behaves. (He wears an ornate ringmaster's jacket, boots, and a tall hat. He has a friendly face, a pleasant voice, but walks and speaks with authority.) Discuss with students why the playwright added these stage directions. What does this description say about death? (Students might say that death is formal but not fearful, and that we all must submit to it.)

- Encourage students to read the Ringmaster's lines and discuss what they might imply about death. For example, the Ringmaster says that he has come to take Dancing Bear "to the Great Center Ring." This line might suggest that the author thinks death has a purpose, or that there is life after death.

- Initiate a discussion of the ways in which different characters respond to the Ringmaster. Ask students what they think their own response would be, and why.

For Performance

- To help students get a feel for the play, present a sample of some of the music mentioned in the script. (See Asides). Encourage students to dance or move in response to the music.

- Group students into small workshops to devise movements for each of the characters in the play and a voice for all but the Mime. (You may want to allow the Mime to use some sounds, such as a whistle or horn.) Encourage each group to try out a wide variety of sounds and mannerisms. Point out that the movements and sound of each character will have an effect on the others. For example, a confident, booming Ringmaster will inspire a different response from the bear than a soft-spoken, cuddly Ringmaster. Invite each team to give a reading of the characters as they conceived them.

Asides

Sound

- A megaphone or portable speaker with microphone will enhance the Announcer's voice.
- Find as many different types of music mentioned in the play as you can—Spanish, calliope, tarantella, etc. (See CDs listed at right.) Choose a student to be the sound engineer for the duration of the class or the entire play, and to employ music as needed.

Dance

Ask a local dance instructor (or perhaps a P.E. teacher) to come in and give students a demonstration of the various dances mentioned: soft shoe, waltz, polka, etc. Ask the dance instructor to draw shoe prints of dance steps on a piece of paper; duplicate and distribute copies to the students.

CDs

- *Music for All Occasions.* (K-Tel International USA, Inc., 1991)
- *Strict Tempo: Ballroom Standard and Latin Dances.* (Baur Productions)

Assessment

The Arkansaw Bear

Reading

Below you will find a list of characters and a list of objects associated with those characters. Match the number of the character with the letter(s) of the objects. Three characters will have more than one object and three objects will go with more than one character.

1. Tish	a. jacket and boots
2. Mime	b. swing
3. Arkansaw Bear	c. tree
4. Dancing Bear	d. turkey feather
5. Grandpa	e. pink flowers
6. Star Bright	f. fishing pole
7. Ringmaster	g. Russian hat
	h. coat with patch pockets
	· i. traveling hat

Writing

Write a poem based on your reading of *The Arkansaw Bear.*

_____

_____

_____

_____

_____

_____

_____

_____

_____

_____

_____

Performance

Choose one of the following performance activities.

• Show the class the steps for one of the dances in the play.

• Choose a favorite activity and mime it for the class.

• Sing one of the songs in the play for your classmates.

The Dancers

Plot Summary

Emily's mother, Elizabeth, and Horace's sister, Inez, have arranged for the two teenagers to attend a dance together. Inez wants Horace to go out with "the prettiest girl in Harrison." Elizabeth does not approve of Emily's chosen beau, Leo. That evening, Emily refuses to go to the dance with Horace, despite her mother's pleas. The next day, Emily apologizes to Horace and introduces him to her friend Mary Catherine. Horace asks Mary Catherine to an upcoming dance, and Mary Catherine agrees to go. Meanwhile, Emily's mother convinces her to go with Horace to the next dance. Inez insists, over her husband's objections, that Horace drop Mary Catherine in favor of Emily. Horace refuses. He goes to Mary Catherine's house, only to be overwhelmed by a lack of confidence. Mary Catherine confesses her own lack of confidence, and the two agree to go to the dance anyway, finding courage and confidence in each other.

The Play as Literature: Plot

The plot of a play generally moves from conflict to crisis to climax to resolution. Yet this pattern can be structured in many ways. The two most common patterns are the climactic and the episodic.

Climactic structure uses a cause-effect pattern in which one action or event leads to another, until the climactic event occurs. *Oedipus Rex* and other Greek plays have a climactic structure. Episodic structure takes the characters on a journey through time and space. The ending remains open until the very end. Many of Shakespeare's and Brecht's plays are episodic.

The Play as Theatre: Movement

Reassure students that becoming aware of movement often makes actors awkward at first. Yet movement helps define character, and physical awareness can help actors make their characters more believable. Allow one or more volunteers to impersonate a person well known to the class. Urge the impersonator to use movement rather than voice to perform the impersonation. You may want to also remind them not to imitate anyone in such a way as to cause hurt feelings.

WARM UP!
Direct students to begin slowly, with broad leg and arm movements that are easy to mimic. As students progress, encourage them to add smaller, quicker movements to their repertoire.

The Dancers

Responding to the Play

1. Most students will probably identify with Mary Catherine and feel an affinity for her. Some may feel the pull of Emily's vivacious personality. Many may believe they could be friends with both.

2. The turning point in the play is the moment Horace stands up to his sister and says, "I am not taking Emily Crews." It could also be argued that the moment Mary Catherine and Horace decide to attend the dance in spite of their fears is a turning point for both of them. The turning point is resolved by Horace picking up Mary Catherine and going off with her to the dance.

3. Mary Catherine might describe her feelings of embarrassment at referring to Horace as a "bore." She also might describe Horace as sweet and easy to talk to. Horace might describe Mary Catherine's upbeat personality, honesty, openness, and apparent confidence.

4. Some students may feel that these characters seem extremely innocent or naive. Others will note that the characters suffer from familiar emotions: fear, embarrassment, anger, the need to make their own decisions, and the need to find friendship and respect.

5. Students should demonstrate body language that reflects the character's emotional response to being stood up.

For Further Discussion

1. Why do you think Inez and Elizabeth want Horace and Emily to go to the dance? *(Inez and Elizabeth would like to continue their ties into the next generation; they think they know what is best for the young people.)*

2. How would you characterize Emily? *(Some students may see her as gracious and dignified; others as stubborn and somewhat selfish. Students should recognize her popularity and her loyalty to her boyfriend and her mother.)*

3. What does Herman mean when he says, "Leave the boy alone. He'll be all right."? *(He is telling his wife that he knows she has good intentions, but she should stop interfering. He also means that Horace's difficulties are normal.)*

Creating and Performing

1. To avoid simple readings of existing dialogue, direct the students to summarize the conflict and describe what each character wants from the other. Encourage them to improvise in contemporary language.

2. Encourage students to develop a series of dance steps first, and then to plan added missteps. Point out that even the missteps must be choreographed.

3. Have students work in pairs to develop a series of letters with two distinct voices. Urge students to create letters that reflect movement and change in the relationship over time.

Presenting the Play

For Reading

- Explain to the students that this play has a climactic structure in which one event leads to another. The first scene provides a narrative about events leading up to the opening of the play. In that scene, Inez reveals that her brother is coming to town for a visit and that she and Elizabeth have been planning his social life without consulting him or his counterpart, Emily. Encourage students to make predictions about plot development by telling how this action by Inez and Elizabeth might affect Horace and Emily. Remember that predictions need not be accurate, as long as they are well-supported by events in the play.

- To highlight the irrevocable nature of events in a climactic structure, encourage students to discuss how the play might have changed under each of the following circumstances:
  - Inez agrees not to interfere.
  - Emily refuses to cooperate from the outset.
  - Emily goes out with Horace.
  - Mary Catherine refuses Horace's invitation to the dance.
  - Horace agrees to stand Mary Catherine up.

- Encourage students to fill out a cause/effect chain for the events in this play as they read. Direct them to circle the climactic event and the resolution. Ask them to choose a partner and read a few lines for the events they have circled.

For Performance

- Point out to the students that the three high-school students in this play have three distinct personalities. Have students read to page 36, where all three characters meet at the drugstore. Ask them to describe each of the three characters and discuss the reason why each one went to the drugstore. Invite volunteers to imagine themselves in the role of one or more characters. One at a time, have them leave the room and take on the role of the character they chose. Then ask them to walk back into the classroom as if it were the drugstore and sit down. Challenge the rest of the students to observe the performer and then tell which character they think is being portrayed and why. Urge students to explain what they would infer about the character from the way he or she walked and sat down.

- Explain to the students that Horace is learning to dance but is not certain of his ability. Ask students how they would portray ability and lack of confidence at the same time? Encourage students to demonstrate their ideas by acting them out.

Asides

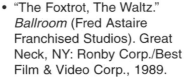

More About *The Dancers*
This play was first produced in 1954 as a television play on Philco Television Playhouse. Joanne Woodward played the role of Emily Crews, and James Broderick played Horace.

Dance
You may want to teach students the waltz or fox trot. The following instructional videos are readily available on VHS.

- "The Foxtrot, The Waltz." *Ballroom* (Fred Astaire Franchised Studios). Great Neck, NY: Ronby Corp./Best Film & Video Corp., 1989.
- "Fox Trot." *Let's Learn How to Dance* (Kathy Blake Dance Studios). Antrim, NH: Butterfly Video.
- "Waltz." *Let's Learn How to Dance* (Kathy Blake Dance Studios). Antrim, NH:

Butterfly Video.

Music
The play calls for dance music to which actors can fox trot or waltz. The following recording is readily available on compact disc: *Waltzes, by Johann Strauss.* Hayes, Middlesex, England: EMI, 1991.

Assessment

The Dancers

Reading

Below you will find ten lines from the play. Identify whether the line belongs to the **rising action** of the play, the **climax,** or the **resolution** by writing **ra, c,** or **r.**

_____ 1. What are you wearing tonight, Emily?

_____ 2. You gave me confidence and I gave you confidence.

_____ 3. Does Horace have a car for tonight?

_____ 4. I don't want to take Emily, I want to take Mary Catherine, and that's just what I'm going to do.

_____ 5. Well, will you go with me?

_____ 6. I didn't want to get out of it, Mary Catherine. I wanted to take you.

_____ 7. You see all you need is confidence.

_____ 8. You're the first girl I've ever really been able to talk to.

_____ 9. I'm ready to go if you are, Mary Catherine.

_____ 10. For my sake, for your sister's sake, you've got to get out of this date with Mary Catherine Davis.

Writing

Inez and Elizabeth went to great lengths to bring Horace and Emily together, but they failed. How do you think they feel about it? Imagine that Inez and Elizabeth meet the next morning. Write a dialogue between the two. If necessary, continue the dialogue on a separate sheet of paper.

_____

_____

_____

_____

_____

_____

_____

_____

Performance

Perform one of the following activities in a manner appropriate to the character performing it.

- Waitress serving a table of four in one trip.
- Horace learning a new dance.
- Emily descending the stairs in a new dress to meet her boyfriend Leo.

Novio Boy

Plot Summary

Rudy, a ninth grader, confides to his best friend Alex that he likes an eleventh grader named Patricia. He has asked her out for a lunch date at Steaks, Steaks, y Mas Steaks. He needs advice on how to behave and money to pay for the meal. Rudy gets advice and loans from friends and family. In the meantime, Patricia has her hair done at a local beauty salon. By chance, her stylist is Rudy's mother, who offers advice and worries aloud that she is losing her son. Rudy meets Patricia for lunch, and sees that his Uncle Juan is working there as a musician. Then Rudy discovers that more of his family and friends are there, including his mother. Nevertheless, the date is a success. As the play ends, Rudy prepares to sell some prized childhood possessions in order to pay off his loans.

The Play as Literature: Characterization

Explain to students that ancient plays often included stock characters, which stood for attitudes, emotions, and principles, such as good and evil. Most plays today feature complex realistic characters, whom we expect to act as real people do in real life. They have hopes and fears, good qualities and bad. Sometimes, one character may even exhibit opposing traits, depending on the circumstances.

To help students get an idea of what a complex character might be like, write on the chalkboard a list of traits (i.e. bashful, outgoing, selfish, generous, suspicious, easy-going, happy, proud, fearful). Ask students to write down the traits that they have shown at some time in their lives. (Students will probably list many of the traits you have written, as well as others.) Then ask them to place an asterisk next to the traits they show most often. Point out that the differences between people—and characters—begin to emerge in the items they chose to asterisk.

The Play as Theatre: The Set

Explain to the students that the set includes the total environment in which the characters find themselves. In a theatrical set, the background is called the scenery. Large items and pieces of furniture that are essential to the set are called set pieces, and these are built by the set crew. Small, portable items that characters use are called props. Props are treated differently from the set.

WARM UP!

If time permits, follow up on this activity by inviting students to role play the meetings discussed, as well as others between enemies, strangers, and acquaintances of various ages. Allow the class to brainstorm a history for each pair of actors before they role play their meeting.

Novio Boy

Responding to the Play

1. Students' answers will vary, but should reflect a knowledge of details in the scene and an understanding of the characters.
2. The characters in the play are largely realistic, in that their motivations are logical and understandable, and their concerns are normal for their ages and circumstances. Nevertheless, some students may feel that the characters are either flat or "too good to be true."
3. Alex, Rudy's mother, Estela, Uncle Juan, and Alicia all care about Rudy and/or Patricia, and all seem capable of giving at least some good advice. Rudy also gives good advice—to the old man. The value of each character's advice is limited by his or her particular concerns.
4. Answers will vary, but should reflect an understanding of the scene chosen.
5. The following elements would probably be essential. Scene 1: two lawn chairs; Scene 2: sofa, magazine; Scene 3: weights, jump rope, squeeze bottle; Scene 4: studio pieces, such as wheeled chair and table; Scene 5: beauty-shop chair, hair dryer; Scene 6: apple display; Scene 7: four tables with chairs, stool. Suggest that students allow for places where each character can sit, stand, walk, and perform the actions required by the play.

For Further Discussion

1. Who in this play do you think gives the best advice about love? Who gives the worst? *(Answers will vary.)*
2. Patricia says she likes Rudy because he is honest. Do you think she is correct or not? Use examples from the play to support your answer. *(Students may focus on Rudy's denial of his relatives at the restaurant, or they may focus on his confessions regarding GI Joe and his bicycle license.)*
3. Do you think Patricia will go out with Rudy again? Why or why not? *(Students may focus on Patricia's kiss and compliment, or they may focus on the fact that she caught him in a lie and that she left the restaurant alone.)*

Creating and Performing

1. Remind students that Mama Rosa and El Gato have distinct radio personalities. El Gato tries to be macho and cool; Mama Rosa is mystical and folksy. Direct them to develop answers that fit those personalities.
2. Possibilites include: be yourself, ask about her likes and dislikes, be polite, keep a sense of humor, be honest, etc.
3. To help students develop specificity in their moments, ask them to think about the image each character wants to present to the world. You may want to provide prompts such as the following.
   • How would this character hold his or her head?
   • What would the character do with his or her hands?
   • What shoes is the character wearing?

Presenting the Play

For Reading

- Before reading, ask for a show of hands from students who know or are studying Spanish. Go through the text and have Spanish-speaking students read aloud the Spanish words and phrases. Invite volunteers to give English definitions or equivalents for the Spanish in the play. Challenge the class as a whole to try out the Spanish pronunciations.

- Remind students that the characters in this contemporary play are meant to be lifelike and realistic. Encourage students to imagine themselves in the roles of Rudy and Patricia. Ask them to think about their own family members and friends who could stand in for Uncle Juan, Mama Rosa, Estela, El Gato, Alex, Alicia, and even the waiter.

- Note that the conflicts in this play are mild, but they still move the action forward. Ask students to jot down each of the conflicts they encounter as they read. *(Students will probably note a conflict between Rudy and his mother, a conflict between his love of childhood toys and his desire to go out on a date, among others.)*

For Performance

- Remind the students that this play has seven scenes, and that each scene takes place in a different setting. Explain that scenery and set pieces can be expensive to buy or time-consuming to make. In addition, long scene changes interrupt the flow of a play and keep audience members from getting involved. As a result, many contemporary set designers create sets by placing a few key pieces on a bare stage. For example, a length of fence can suggest a backyard. Encourage students to think about and discuss simple scenery or set pieces that could define each scene in this play.

- Point out to the students that each setting in the play provides information about the circumstances, habits, and personality of one or more characters. For example, Alex hangs out with Rudy in his backyard and helps him out with a sale in his front yard. Clearly, Alex is a close, personal friend. Encourage students to identify each character's "place" or "places" and explain what those settings tell about the characters.

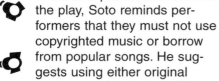

Asides

           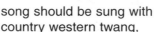

Music

In his own production notes for the play, Soto reminds performers that they must not use copyrighted music or borrow from popular songs. He suggests using either original music or music in the public domain. He also offers the following ideas:

- In Scene 3, Uncle Juan's song should be sung with a country western twang, probably employing G, A, and D chords.
- In scene 4, the song should be sung with either a rap or a ranchera beat.

Writing

References to Fresno, California, may be changed to local references. References to well-known people and places also may be changed for local appeal.

Costumes

To accomplish the change in Estela's hair color, hide a wig in the hair dryer. Direct the actor playing Estela to pull the wig on secretly, as she pretends to check her hair for dryness.

Assessment

Novio Boy

Reading

Based on what you know about the characters, match each quote to the person who said it.

a. Rudy
b. Alex
c. Patricia

d. Rudy's Mother
e. Uncle Juan
f. El Gato

g. Mama Rosa
h. Estela
i. Old Man

j. Waiter

_____ 1. Just level with her. Tell her you're sorry you look like you do.

_____ 2. A Chicano hippie, *lo mejor,* the best.

_____ 3. You got to stop your nonsense. It's about time you got a regular job.

_____ 4. Dance? No, I'm too full. Those crackers filled me up.

_____ 5. What is love but some spring in your legs and a combination plate from El Pollo Loco?

_____ 6. I ain't got an attitude! How come everyone thinks I got an attitude?

_____ 7. I like him because he's honest.

_____ 8. You don't have to please me. It's the boss. She expects you to bring in a crowd.

_____ 9. Now, about potions. I recommend a simple one.

_____ 10. To be frank, I'm just a boring guy.

Writing

Write lyrics for a song, in English or Spanish, that Juan can sing at Steaks, Steaks, Y Mas Steaks. If you wish, compose the music, as well.

_____

_____

_____

_____

_____

Performance

Choose one of the following activities to perform.

- Sing and/or play the song you composed in the writing section of this assessment page.

- Imagine you are a disc jockey on a radio talk show. Write your own "questions from callers" and perform a show in which you read the questions and answer them using your radio personality.

- Perform a phone monologue in which Patricia describes her date with Rudy.

The Man in a Case

Plot Summary

In a small Russian town, Varinka has come to visit her betrothed, Byelinkov. She enters the garden, and the two begin to talk about their marriage. Byelinkov is interested in responsibility, and Varinka is concerned with happiness. Varinka persuades Byelinkov to dance, and he places a sprig of lilac in her hair. Joyously, they discuss household details and their love. When Byelinkov discovers that Varinka has ridden her brother's bicycle in order to pay this visit, he becomes distraught and worried about what people will think. He tries to ride the bicycle in order to return it, but his garments get tangled in the works. Varinka can't help but laugh, and Byelinkov's pride is injured. He sends Varinka away so he can return to his work. Varinka leaves, still looking forward to a life with Byelinkov. Byelinkov, however, has already begun to speak as if their relationship is in the past.

The Play as Literature: Diction

Explain to students that the choice between formal and informal language is another component of diction. The woman in this play uses informal metaphors and exclamations, while the man uses more formal language and more adjectives. Make sure students understand that *denotation* means the actual definition of a word, and *connotation* is a word's emotional value. In order to make the distinction more concrete, discuss with students the different connotative meanings of several synonymous words, such as *dirt, soil,* and *earth.*

The Play as Theatre: Listening and Reacting

Point out to students that body language can communicate as much or more than speech. An actor can communicate through facial expression, the set of the head, general posture, and gesture. Effective performers are aware of all these elements when they play a scene.

WARM UP! Explain to students that the purpose of the repetition exercise is to practice paying full attention to one's partner. It will help them learn to listen to words and intonations, watch expressions, and feel their own immediate reactions to what others say. Encourage the pairs to continue repeating a single phrase without attempting to vary it, but to allow variations that escape unbidden. Point out that those "true" reactions are the basis of realistic acting.

The Man in a Case

Responding to the Play

1. Students' answers will vary but should be based on the reasoning and perceptions they share with the characters.
2. Students' answers should reflect a recognition that Byelinkov is laconic, judgmental, and rather unemotional, while Varinka is effusive, rather unfocused, and emotional. They seem to like one another, but don't seem to understand one another very well.
3. Byelinkov sees his galoshes as a necessary protective garment and the bicycle as a dangerous innovation. Varinka sees the galoshes as an endearing eccentricity and the bicycle as an opportunity to have an adventure.
4. Students will most likely conclude that Byelinkov has decided to discard the relationship in a tidy way. Alternatively, they may argue that he tries, but fails, to get rid of his compulsion for tidy note taking.
5. Students might respond that they would react with anger, frustration, ridicule, or protectiveness. Encourage them to defend their answers using clues from the text of the play.

For Further Discussion

1. How does Varinka show her affection for Byelinkov? *(She calls him a pet, a school mouse, a dancing bear, and a stale babka; she brags about her cooking; she declares that they will be happy.)*
2. How does Byelinkov show his affection for Varinka? *(He muses about his responsibility to her; he puts a lilac sprig in her hair.)*
3. How does Byelinkov's attitude regarding laughter differ from that of Varinka? *(Byelinkov laughs at his own joke, but otherwise associates laughter with ridicule. Varinka seems to consider it harmless fun.)*

Creating and Performing

1. Have students try out the endings they write by asking classmates to perform readings. Direct the readers and writers to discuss the parts of the rewrite that they particularly like as well as any areas that seem problematic. Encourage these small groups to work together as a team to revise and perform the new ending.
2. Encourage students to break down the movements in this activity into small, manageable bits, then to put the bits together to mime the scene.
3. Remind students to remain focused on the individual preferences of the characters and the fact that they plan to marry. Urge students to think about what their characters want from each other in this particular passage.

Presenting the Play

For Reading

- To reinforce the way in which language expresses character, have students look for and record the exaggerations Varinka makes and the judgments Byelinkov imposes. Challenge students, as they read, to locate the moment in which Byelinkov seems to change his plans as regards Varinka.

- Both characters in the play utter the line, "We deserve not to be different," yet for each it has a different meaning. Have students interpret that line for each character, then read the line aloud as one of the characters.

- Point out that the characters in this play listen to each other only occasionally. More often, they speak in response to their own fantasies and fears. Challenge students to highlight or list the times when one character is actually responding to the words of the other.

- Explain to the students that, like Chekhov, Wasserstein composed her dialogue to be somewhat neutral. As a result, actors can color the scenes with their own interpretation of the lines. Ask two volunteers to represent Byelinkov and Varinka. Have the class suggest each character's state of mind (i.e. anxious, giddy, judgmental, sentimental) during a particular moment in the play. The volunteers play the scene using the suggested emotions of their character.

For Performance

- Most schools will not have on hand an old-fashioned bicycle. Directors can choose to provide a simple balloon-tire bicycle, a cardboard mock-up, or any semblance of a bicycle they can find.

- Restrictive clothing can help students gain insight into the constraints of the time. Girls should wear high-heeled boots; layers of long, heavy skirts; and tight, highneck collars. They should wear their hair in a bun. Boys should wear spectacles, close fitting shirts, bow ties, wool jackets, and slacks.

- The 1890s and early 1900s were a much more formal time than today. Restrictions on language and behavior limited how people expressed themselves, but not how they felt. People experienced the same range of emotions we do today, including wild hopes and crippling fears. Encourage students to act their roles as naturally as possible, despite the restrictions placed on their characters.

- Stage directions for this play call for a fade to black. This can be achieved using a simple dimmer switch. If a fade is impossible to provide, you might direct students to slow and then freeze their actions before you pull a curtain or provide a blackout.

Asides

Playwright's Corner
Anton Chekhov is best known for his full-length plays, such as *The Seagull* (1896), *Uncle Vanya* (1899), *The Three Sisters* (1901), and *The Cherry Orchard* (1904). Also available is *Orchards, Orchards, Orchards: Plays.* NY: Broadway Play Publishing, Inc., 1987, which contains seven plays

based on Chekhov's stories.

Wendy Wasserstein is a well-regarded contemporary playwright whose works include *Uncommon Women and Others, The Heidi Chronicles, The Sisters Rosensweig,* and *An American Daughter.* She wrote the screenplay for the 1998 film *Isn't It Romantic?* Wasserstein

won both the Pulitzer Prize for Drama and the Tony Award in 1989 for her play *The Heidi Chronicles.*

Stories by Anton Chekhov
Chekhov's stories are readily available in numerous anthologies. The translation of "The Man in a Case," from which this play was adapted, came from *Stories of Russian Life.*

Assessment

The Man in a Case

Reading

Identify each of the lines below as **formal** or **informal.** You may want to underline the key word or words to help support your evaluation.

_____ 1. She adores you!

_____ 2. She is emotionally loose.

_____ 3. You speak about me as if I were your pet.

_____ 4. You are my pet! My little school mouse.

_____ 5. We had a good giggle.

_____ 6. That is not progressive, it is a premeditated revolutionary act.

_____ 7. She is a potato-vending sausage-armed fool!

_____ 8. Allow me to help you onto your bicycle.

_____ 9. Ha, ha, ha! My little school mouse. You look so funny!

_____ 10. Shhh!

Writing

Imagine that Byelinkov and Varinka meet at the market the next day. Write a scene between them.

_____
_____
_____
_____
_____
_____
_____
_____
_____
_____
_____

Performance

Choose one of the following activities to perform.

• Varinka returns the apricots to the grocery woman.

• Varinka returns her brother's bicycle

• Your written exchange between Byelinkov and Varinka at the market.

Variations on the Death of Trotsky

Plot Summary

Leon Trotsky, a leader of the Russian Revolution of 1917, was exiled by Stalin in 1924. He and his wife fled to Mexico, and in 1941 Trotsky was slain by his gardener, who killed him with an axe blow to the head. Playwright David Ives presents eight variations on a scene in which Trotsky realizes he has been killed.

In Variation One, Mrs. Trotsky reads an encyclopedia entry detailing her husband's murder by their gardener, Ramon Mercader. Trotsky responds that the capitalist press never gets things right, but Mrs. Trotsky points out that there is, indeed, a mountain-climber's axe in his skull. He looks in the mirror, realizes the truth, and dies. Variations Two through Five move along in much the same way, with Trotsky denying reality and Mrs. Trotsky stating the obvious. Variations Six and Seven explore comic plot developments that might explain Trotsky's death. Variation Eight pokes fun at philosophical and historical interpretations of the event.

The Play as Literature: Irony

Explain to students that a writer uses irony to surprise an audience and keep it involved. The writer assumes we will have certain expectations and plays on them. Then he or she turns the tables on us. Some writers, like Ives, use irony in order to create humor. Others employ dramatic or tragic irony to create suspense or to comment on events.

Discuss with students the ironic moments in the first variation. Include the following: Trotsky learning about himself through an encyclopedia; Trotsky complaining about the inaccuracies of the "capitalist press," which prove to be correct; Trotsky dying only after he reads that he is dead.

Point out that Variations Two through Eight build on and add to the ironies in the first variation. Encourage students to identify further ironies in each variation. For example, in Variation Two, Trotsky argues in favor of force, but it is force that kills him.

The Play as Theatre: Burlesque

To help students better understand burlesque, show a film or video of the form in action, such as *This Is Spinal Tap* or *A Night at the Opera,* starring the Marx Brothers. Discuss how the writer or director of the film mocks or exaggerates the qualities of the subject and how the performers interpret this exaggeration.

Have students create a list of celebrities. Ask them to identify a distinguishing characteristic for each, such as a physical feature, mannerism, or speech habit. An example might be Arnold Schwartzenegger's accent. Point out also that some celebrities cultivate identifying features, such as the face paint and glam-rock clothing of the band Kiss. Still others try to associate themselves with a powerful slogan, as exemplified by political candidates.

WARM UP! Have students pair off and read each other the lines they wrote. Then ask each pair to choose one of the lines and develop a short scene. Point out that variations in tone and context can create humor in a scene.

Variations on the Death of Trotsky

Responding to the Play

1. Students should give thoughtful explanations for their choices.
2. Students might touch on ironic elements such as: Mrs. Trotsky's matter-of-fact discussions with a husband who sports an axe in his head, Trotsky's defense of the proletariat despite being murdered by his gardener, Trotsky's regret over missing some of the highlights of capitalist culture.
3. Students' answers will vary.
4. In Variation One, Trotsky is full of himself and persistent in the belief that the capitalist press's reports of his death are greatly exaggerated. In Variation Eight, he is apologetic about his past, philosophical, and hopeful about his death.
5. Each student's additional variation should be unique, but probably should include Trotsky, Mrs. Trotsky, and perhaps Mercader; a comic tone; and Trotsky dying at the end.

For Further Discussion

1. In what ways does Trotsky try to avoid the fate outlined for him in the encyclopedia? (He denies the truthfulness of the media, and tries to offer a substitute skull.)
2. How would you characterize Trotsky's attitude toward the press? (He is ambivalent. He believes the capitalist press can't be trusted, yet he dies the moment he reads he is dead. He decries the power of the printed word, yet he writes to disseminate his ideas.)
3. Based on the way Mrs. Trotsky is presented in the play, how would you characterize her? (Answers may take into account her support, sense of humor, irreverence, occasional show of strength, pragmatism, and involvement with her husband's fate.)

Creating and Performing

1. Encourage students to create a characteristic movement, speech pattern, or gesture for each character. Remind them that the characteristics they choose should offer information about the character. For example, Trotsky's movements might signify commitment, intensity, intellectualism, or absentmindedness.
2. If students have difficulty thinking up puns, allow them to invent new dialogue using the puns in the play.
3. If time permits, invite students to cast their version, rehearse it with classmates, and perform it for the rest of the class.

Presenting the Play

For Reading

- The word *burlesque* is from the Italian *burla,* meaning a joke. It is a form that allows a playwright's comic imagination to run wild. Discuss burlesque with students in terms of David Ives' play. Point out the deviations from the norm in the behavior and speech of each of the characters, particularly Trotsky. Suggest to students that they choose a partner and read a favorite scene with a friend, trying to convey the humor while still giving a serious reading.

- Help students understand burlesque firsthand by asking them to find a current news item that could become a burlesque scene. Encourage them to identify what makes this news item worthy of treatment as a burlesque.

- Writers throughout history have employed the burlesque form, including Spanish author Miguel de Cervantes, French playwright Molière, and British collaborators Gilbert and Sullivan, creators of many lighthearted operettas. You might want to share one or two of these artists' works with your students. Also invite students to share readings from works they consider burlesque.

For Performance

- To help students explore the physical nature of acting, encourage them to watch how people walk as they go about their daily lives. Point out that some people seem to lead with the head, particularly the nose or chin. Others thrust their shoulders, chest, belly, or hips in front of them as they walk. Some people even seem to lead with their knees or feet. Then, ask students to demonstrate these various walks, letting classmates describe the kind of characters who might walk this way.

- Ask students to chose a scene or variation from the play and identify its humorous aspects. Then invite students to practice their comic timing and characterization by reading the scene. Encourage quirky interpretations, exaggerated emotions, and broad gestures.

- Point out to students that comedy often requires actors to be serious while their characters are funny or even ridiculous. Discuss techniques the actor might use to focus on the comic routine without laughing.

Asides

Other Plays by David Ives
- *All in the Timing: Fourteen Plays,* Vintage, 1995.
- *Ancient History,* Dramatist's Play Service.

Media Links
- The classic comedy routine "Who's on First" by Abbott and Costello, a skit in the tradition of American burlesque, can be found on audiocassette from Metacom, available in many bookstores and from Amazon.com.

- A videocassette of Ives' play *Long Ago and Far Away,* 1995, from L.A. Theatre Works, can be special ordered from Amazon.com.

Costuming
- The most prominent object in this play is the axe protruding from Trotsky's head. Students can create this costume piece by creating a prop axe out of cardboard. They can then paint the blade silver and the handle brown, and glue the

entire piece to a wig.

Blackouts
- Comic scenarios like those in this play often end in a "blackout." Traditionally, such scenes end when the stage lights go quickly to black. In this play and some others, a bell rings and stops the action. Some contemporary plays end when characters freeze and a stagehand simply yells "blackout!"

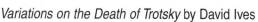

Assessment

Variations on the Death of Trotsky

Reading

Below is a list of lines from the play. Read each line and underline the words or phrases that contribute to the play's comic irony.

1. What is the year of that encyclopedia?

2. Then I'm safe. The article says it happened on the twentieth, which means it would've happened yesterday.

3. No one is safe. Force must be used.

4. Is it the *Britannica?*

5. A mountain-climber's axe! *A mountain-climber's axe!* CAN'T I GET THAT THROUGH YOUR SKULL?

6. Have you been oppressing him?

7. Maybe he was just hot-to-trotsky.

8. Do you think you will have time to look at the nasturtiums today? They are really very beautiful.

9. Trotsky: Well, it's a little late for regrets, with a mountain-climber's axe buried in one's skull.
   Mrs. Trotsky: Smashed, actually.

10. It gives you a little hope about the world, doesn't it?

Writing

Based on the material in this play, write an obituary for Leon Trotsky.

_____

_____

_____

_____

_____

Performance

Choose one of the following performance activities.

• Demonstrate eight different ways for Trotsky to die.

• Develop a characteristic gesture for one of the characters in the play. Perform a scene from the play using the gesture as a comic element.

• Perform this play as a radio play, with sound effects instead of actions.

A Conversation with My Dogs

Plot Summary

A woman identified only as "Me" calls for her dogs in order to tell them that they need not follow her everywhere she goes. The dogs, Bob and Stan, are incredulous and hurt. They agree, however, not to follow her when she goes to get tissue. "What's your position on pens?" Bob wonders. The woman wants the dogs to admit that they only follow her because they think there might be a chance of getting food. The dogs deny this and suggest that they do hope it might turn into a game of ball. They then accuse her of starving them to death. She tells them again not to bother following her. She will only feed them once a day, and she will tell them when she wants to play ball. The woman then gets up to find her purse. The dogs scamper after her in hopes of getting food.

The Play as Literature: Tone

Encourage students to discuss what they know about tone by asking them whether they've ever been criticized for the tone they've employed when speaking to parents or other authorities. Help students create a list of elements that influence tone (volume, speed, word choice, varying emphasis on individual words or phrases, body language).

Point out that plays, like other works of literature, make use of tone in several ways. The overall tone of a work signals the author's attitude and expectations. Yet characters within a story or play may offer supplementary, or even conflicting tones—much as a painting includes many various shades of color. Thus, different actors in a play may employ different tones to establish and distinguish their characters. The same character's tone might change in response to new conditions.

The Play as Theatre: Physicalization

Point out to students that awareness of posture, gesture, and facial expression can give an actor tools for expressing character, but that these tools must not devolve into crutches. One can no more express a character solely through physical attributes than one can express a character while calling from behind a curtain. Effective actors let the reality of the play and the emotional life of the characters inform and direct their physical interpretations. Still, physical awareness can help an actor fill in details about the characters he or she plays. Early in the rehearsal process, an actor might find the following questions helpful:

- What is my character's overall stance? (Examples: proud, timid, rigid, relaxed, open, closed, belligerent, fearful, etc.)

- When walking, does my character lead with a particular part of the body? (Characters might lead with the forehead, chin, chest, belly, pelvis, knees, or feet.)

- Does my character have a characteristic way of moving? (Sweeping gestures as opposed to small, tight movements.)

- What is my character's overall approach to life? (Characters may tend to be hopeful, joyful, worried, fearful, sly, or explosive.)

Playing an animal requires additional physical practice and study. One actor might play an animal as humanlike, using makeup and stylized movements. Another will try to reproduce the animal's real movements.

WARM UP!
Suggest that students base their portrayals on the mood or reaction the object provokes in them. For example, a lamp might seem intense, mysterious, helpful, or flamboyant, depending on its style and use. Encourage them to develop a posture, gesture, and facial expression to define the "character" of the object.

A Conversation with My Dogs

Responding to the Play

1. Students' biographies of "Me," Stan, and Bob should be in keeping with the reading—lighthearted and fun.
2. Programs will vary according to each student's ability. Each program should include a cover, a list of characters and actors, and a list of production staff.
3. Most students will describe the tone as tongue-in-cheek, lighthearted, funny, offbeat, or even silly. Examples should come from the text of the play.
4. Bob and Stan's physicality should include such doglike behaviors as bounding around on all fours, panting, sitting on hind legs, scratching, stretching on all fours, licking, looking very intently at the speaker, curling up, lying with the chin resting on the floor, etc.
5. Bob's complaints should probably include such things as never getting fed, being insulted, being underappreciated, never getting to play ball, having to put up with Stan, etc.

For Further Discussion

1. How are Stan and Bob different from each other? What characteristics do they share? *(Bob tends to be bumbling and evasive; Stan is more intelligent and confrontational. Both have the same interest in acquiring food and maintaining the good will of their human.)*
2. How do the dogs differ from the human? *(The dogs think in terms of immediate gratification. The human looks ahead.)*
3. What do the last two lines suggest about Stan and Bob? *(They suggest that Stan and Bob have not been listening, don't understand, or prefer not to believe the human.)*

Creating and Performing

1. Help students be specific in their choices by suggesting that they portray a particular breed of dog, or even a dog they know personally.
2. Direct students to use stage directions as a way to highlight a character's response, signal a new development in plot, or add humor to a situation.
3. Encourage students who are portraying the dogs' movements to identify the clues to character that each physical movement provides.

Presenting the Play

For Reading

- To reinforce how differences in tone affect meaning, allow students to play a game of "Don't Speak to Me in That Tone." Have students choose one or more lines from the play and say them to a partner. The partner responds, "Don't speak to me in that tone." The first student must respond by presenting the line in a new way. Partners switch roles when a speaker repeats a tone he or she has used before.

- Encourage students to explore how the differences in tone between Stan and Bob help define the relationship between the two dogs. Encourage interested students to improvise a conversation that expresses the relationship between the dogs. Also suggest they they develop a voice and attitude that fits each dog.

- Help students gain awareness of physical movements they employ automatically by asking volunteers to stage a scene between Me, Stan, and Bob as if it were a scene between three humans. Invite the rest of the class to take notes on the posture, gestures, and expressions of each character. At the end of the scene, have classmates read their lists to the performers. Lead a discussion of the way in which the physical movements performers used might apply to the characters that are dogs.

For Performance

- Encourage students to perfect their physical understanding of Stan and Bob by observing and mimicking the behavior of dogs. Challenge students to develop human alternatives to a dog's use of its ears and tail. Remind them to use a voice that fits each dog they observe.

- Use the blackline master on page 72 to help students develop a makeup plan for one or more characters in this play. Direct them to consult pictures of dogs and copy them or attach them to their plans. Encourage students to include in their designs any wigs or headwear they think necessary.

- Costuming for this play can be approached in many ways. You might have students create fairly realistic dog costumes. You might prefer that they use leotards, makeup, and small costuming elements to create the illusion of a dog. Or they might rely solely on their acting techniques to create a dog persona.

- If you wish to use this play as an opportunity for a mask workshop, obtain plain masks from a costume store and direct students to alter them. Or encourage students to make papier mâché masks to represent dogs' faces. Caution students to coat their faces with petroleum jelly and to leave breathing holes before applying papier mâché strips to their faces.

Asides

Physical Research
Students can observe dog behavior by taking field trips to local parks or a nearby shelter. Encourage them to take notes, draw pictures, and try out some of the postures and movements they observe.

Across the Curriculum
The following juvenile science book is a lyrical examination of

the world animals inhabit: *The View from the Oak: The Private Worlds of Other Creatures* by Herbert and Judith Kohl, illustrated by Robert Bayless. San Francisco: Sierra Club Books/Scriber's, 1977.
  The Hidden Life of Dogs by Elizabeth Marshall Thomas, Houghton Mifflin, New York,

explains the habits of dogs and the meaning of their various posturings and movements.

Internet
You can download "stupid pet tricks" by Bob Sokol and his dog, Amyl, as they appeared on *Late Show with David Letterman,* at the following internet address: www.bobsokol.com/spt/spt.html

Assessment

A Conversation with My Dogs

Reading

Read the following lines uttered by Stan, Bob, and "Me." Then choose a tone from the list that you think applies to the line as it appears in the play.

a. innocent
b. superior
c. sarcastic

d. reasonable
e. angry
f. sly

_____ 1. We *like* to watch you get Kleenex. We happen to think it's something you do very well.

_____ 2. Is there something wrong with the back fence? I have no idea what happened.

_____ 3. Okay. Fine. No problem. Get your Kleenex alone from now on.

_____ 4. The reason I've summoned you here today is I really think we should talk about something.

_____ 5. You don't listen at all, do you. Going for *pens* means food. She said she's getting her *purse.* That means *ball.*

_____ 6. There's no reason to have hurt feelings.

_____ 7. Very nice manners, by the way.

_____ 8. One bowl of food is a joke. It's an hors d'oeuvre. It does nothing but whet my appetite.

_____ 9. We wouldn't want to you overexert yourself in any way. You have to rest and save up all your strength for all that Kleenex fetching.

_____ 10. Who is she talking to?

Writing

Though Bob and Stan are dogs who have many interests in common, they employ different tones. On a separate sheet of paper, write a conversation in which Stan and Bob use their characteristic tones.

Performance

Choose an activity below to perform. Keep in mind your character's physical aspects.

- Stan gives a lecture/demonstration on sneaking food while humans are gone.
- Stan and Bob quarrel about whose turn it is nap on the couch.
- "Me" gives a class in dog training, using Stan and Bob as "helpers."

He Who Says Yes and He Who Says No

Plot Summary

A young boy's mother is dying and he is determined to take the treacherous journey across the mountain to find the medicine and medical advice she needs. His teacher and three students are making the journey, but the boy is warned not to go. He insists on making the dangerous trek nevertheless. Along the way, the boy becomes ill. He can go no further. The teacher asks him to decide whether everyone should turn back for his sake. However, says the teacher, "Custom demands that you answer: You shall not turn back."

At this point in the play, two different endings are presented. In the first, the boy says, "Yes, I agree." He begs to be thrown into the valley rather than die alone. His wish is granted. In the second ending, the boy responds, "No. I do not agree." The teacher tells him that people will "hurl disgrace" upon him. Nevertheless, he is carried back to town by his friends.

The Play as Literature: Theme

Remind students that a play's theme is its underlying message. Help them differentiate between mood, conflict, and theme by discussing those elements in this play. The mood here is solemn, earnest, and rather dark. The conflict involves the difficult choice the boy must make. The theme rests in the tension between social rules and the rights of the individual. Conflict and mood help build this theme. Help students contrast the theme of acceptance of social rules in *He Who Says Yes* to the theme of overriding rules to find new solutions in *He Who Says No.*

The Play as Theatre: The Chorus

If your class has access to the internet, visit www.iijnet.or.jp/NOH-KYOGEN/index.html for a wealth of information about Noh theatre, including many colorful images of the costumes, masks, and traditional characters. Discuss with students the kinds of Noh masks and costumes that might be employed in Brecht's play.

Ask students to identify bands that use backup singers. Have them enumerate the functions of backup singers *(they sing harmony, fill out the sound, add visual interest, sometimes add additional words).* Compare them to the chorus in this play.

Show students a video of a classical Greek play such as Oedipus Rex or Antigone. Invite students to comment on the function and effect of the Greek chorus. Help students perceive the ways in which the Greek chorus comments on the action. Compare the chorus in *He Who Says Yes and He Who Says No* to the Greek chorus.

WARM UP!
To help students understand how a chorus can affect the tone of a play, have the entire class recite a familiar song or poem in various styles, such as a dirge, an anthem, a cheer, or a party song. Then ask the groups of four who got together earlier to practice and share their readings of the paragraph on page 106.

He Who Says Yes and He Who Says No

Responding to the Play

1. Students' answers will vary. Some will see that the lesson of the play—the great impact that choices have on consequences and the need to choose wisely—is very relevant. Others may find that the situations and the expectation of upholding customs so stringently are too far out of their realm.
2. The boy said yes to the expectations placed upon him, to responding in the honorable way, and to his own death. He said no to tradition, perhaps to his good name, and to his own death.
3. Student designs will vary, but should include two rooms and a platform.
4. Students' observations may be similar to the following: Both groups speak in unison and present a united opinion. However, only the great chorus has more than one role in the play. The chorus narrates ("Then the mother said"), tells the audience what has occurred and is occurring, and encourages the actors. The three students play the same role throughout, that of young men reacting to a distressing situation. The three students respond to the boy's decisions differently in each part of the play. The chorus comments in much the same way in both parts.
5. Descriptions will vary. Some students may costume the chorus in long, colorful Japanese robes, as in Noh theatre. Others may feel that the chorus should wear plain robes or simply pants and shirts. Others may suggest that the chorus wear mountain-climbing garb.

For Further Discussion

1. How do the circumstances around the epidemic in *He Who Says Yes* differ from those in *He Who Says No*? *(In* He Who Says Yes, *the teacher explains immediately that the trip he is taking is to gain medicine and advice. In* He Who Says No, *the teacher says he is going on a "research trip." The boy assumes the trip will procure medicine and advice.)*
2. Did you agree with all, some, or none of the boy's choices? What would you have done in the same circumstances? *(Answers will vary. Students should exhibit some understanding of the boy's plight.)*

Creating and Performing

1. To make this exercise more concrete, you might want to have students perform activities that will produce the state in which characters find themselves. For example, have students run around a track carrying books before saying the lines on page 111.
2. Advise students to consider their own positions on the topic before writing the third ending to the play. Encourage them to create an ending that supports their position in favor of or against saying "perhaps."
3. Point out to students that costuming supports the theme of a play. For example, Japanese costuming would reinforce the play's ties to Noh theatre and Japanese traditions. Contemporary clothing would highlight the theme as a current concern. Colors and fabrics make statements about various characters or roles.

Presenting the Play

For Reading

- Before reading, ask a volunteer to read aloud the title of this play. Invite the class to discuss what the theme might be, based on the play's title. Write student responses on a chalkboard for reference as they read.

- Point out to the students that the characters in this play are known by their roles instead of by individual names. Invite students to think of names for the characters that reflect their functions in the play. For example, the teacher might be named Mr. Convention, Mr. Social Rules, or Mr. Right.

- Explain to students that, in this play, Brecht allows the chorus to spell out the meaning of scenes. Have students sit in groups of three throughout the classroom. Ask them to practice saying the chorus's lines in unison.

For Performance

- Point out to students that classical European theatre, Noh theatre, and Brechtian theatre all include formalized movements. Invite students to demonstrate how the characters in this play might use movement to convey their role, status, and eventual fate.

- You may want to encourage students to choreograph gestures and movements to support the repetition in this play and to add to the ritualistic atmosphere of the scenes. Encourage a team of students to serve as choreographers for each of the choral pronouncements.

- Invite the groups who practiced saying the chorus's lines in unison to present their scene for the class.

Asides

History

Noh theatre was developed in the 1300s in Japan by two actors, a father and son. They created a play form in which beautifully masked and costumed male actors danced and sang or chanted poetic tales based on legend, myth, and Buddhist scriptures. Their movements were choreographed, or preset, to music.

By the 1600s, the training of a Noh actor was firmly fixed. Each actor learned his role from the actor who played it before him, so that his movements and speech would be exactly like those of all the actors before him. By about 1650 Noh theatre was eclipsed by a new theatre form called Kabuki, which featured women performers and emphasized dance. Both Noh and Kabuki are still performed in Japan.

Writing

Have students work in groups of four to six in order to dramatize an everyday conflict, such as the interaction between a teacher and a student who has forgotten to turn in homework. First, direct each group to write a realistic scene between the two people in conflict. Then ask them to add commentary by a chorus. Allow students to make their commentary partial or impartial, somber or humorous.

Media

Students might enjoy these videos on Noh and Kabuki:
Society's Video Letter from Japan: Living Arts, 1988. Developed by Marilyn Turkovich and Linda Babolz for the Asia Society.

Kabuki: Tradition in Today's World (VHS, 30min)

Send a request for JV040 to East Asia Program Resource Lending

Library, Cornell University, 140 Uris Hall, Ithaca, NY 14853; Tel: (607) 255-6222, Fax: (607) 255-1388; email: lad2@cornell.edu. The video is free for educational purposes.

Other Works by Bertolt Brecht

- *Baal, A Man's a Man, & The Elephant Calf,* translated by Martin Esslin. NY: Grove Press, 1989.
- *The Good Person of Szechwan,* translated by Ralph Manheim. NY: Arcade Pub., Inc, 1994.
- *The Life of Galileo, The Restistable Rise of Arturo Uo,* and *The Caucasian Chalk Circle,* translated by Ralph Manheim. NY: Arcade Pub. Inc., 1994.
- *Mother Courage & Her Children,* translated and adapted by Eric Bentley. NY: Grove Press, 1987.
- *The Threepenny Opera,* translated by Ralph Manheim, NY: Arcade Pub., Inc., 1994.

Assessment

He Who Says Yes and He Who Says No

Reading

Some of the lines below belong to *He Who Says Yes*. Some belong to *He Who Says No*. Others belong to **both.** Identify the part of the play to which each line belongs.

_____ 1. An epidemic has broken out among us, and in the city beyond the mountains live some famous doctors.

_____ 2. Many say yes to falsehoods/But he says yes not to illness/But that illness be healed.

_____ 3. We say it with dread but if he cannot go on we will have to leave him here in the mountains.

_____ 4. We can't carry anyone./Should we follow the great custom/And hurl him into the valley?

_____ 5. I'm going on a research trip over the mountains soon. For in the city beyond the mountains live some famous teachers.

_____ 6. You saw that no argument/Could move him.

_____ 7. No, you shall not turn back!

_____ 8. No! I do not agree.

_____ 9. No one more cowardly than his neighbor.

_____ 10. No one guiltier than his neighbor.

Writing

Write two speeches for the Mother: one that fits the ending for *He Who Says Yes* and another that fits the ending for *He Who Says No.*

_____

_____

_____

_____

_____

_____

_____

Performance

Choose one of the following activities.

• Perform one of the monologues you wrote for the Mother.

• With partners, improvise a contemporary version of the play.

• Retell the play as a two-part legend.

I Never Saw Another Butterfly

Plot Summary

During the Holocaust, Nazi Germany systematically murdered millions of Jews. In the early 1940s, thousands of Jewish children lived for a time in a camp in Terezin, Czechoslovakia. This is their story, as told by one of the few survivors, Raja Englanderova. Raja's father had tried to accommodate the Nazis in hope of finding fairness. Her brother, Pavel, had opposed them through civil disobedience. Neither technique proved helpful. The family was rounded up and sent to concentration camps.

In Terezin, Raja meets Irena Synkova, a caring teacher of the children there, and Honza, a young rebel who publishes an underground camp newspaper. She and the other children are given paper to draw and write on and are encouraged to tell their stories. They also find courage and solace in the music they perform. Throughout their incarceration, they see many friends herded off to the death camp of Auschwitz. One day Irena's number is called, and then Honza's. Despite her anguish, Raja remembers the love and bravery of her family and friends and summons the courage to live.

The Play as Literature: Dramatic Monologue

Point out that most plays observe a convention known as the "fourth wall." Actors behave as if the "rooms" in which the scenes take place have four solid walls; the audience peers through the invisible "fourth wall" to view the action. Monologues break the fourth wall, allowing characters to speak directly to the audience.

Explain to the students that dramatic monologues reveal important details about the speaker or the circumstances of the play. Sometimes, they allow a character to share with the audience information that other characters don't know. Thus, monologues can draw the audience further into the action of the play.

If you wish, demonstrate this concept by suddenly turning aside to an invisible audience and explaining what you hope to accomplish in your role as a teacher. Ask students what they discovered from your monologue that they did not know. Encourage them to identify information they gained through your monologue that would not normally be available to them.

The Play as Theatre: Sound

Explain to students that sound designers develop a sound log for plays on which they work. Lead students in developing a sound log for this play. Have them list each act and scene and then indicate the places where specific sounds occur. Point out that wise sound designers list the line on which the sound engineer readies a sound, the line on which the sound is to be activated, and the line in which the sound ends. The reproducible on page 73 shows a typical format for a sound log.

WARM UP!

Explain to students that designers on a budget often suggest simple sounds rather than trying to create exact representations. Challenge them to suggest ways to simulate common sounds, such as running water (*shh* into a microphone), galloping horses (clap wood blocks together), and walking (put shoes on hands and walk them over a wooden tray filled with gravel).

I Never Saw Another Butterfly

Responding to the Play

1. Students may say that while we are alive, even if for a short time, we must do what is right, be strong, and live fully. They may also stress the importance of remembering the past and carrying it into the future.

2. It gives the play a universality. It shows Raja as having come full circle. As a survivor, she has a perspective that no other character in the play can have. She knows the past, is experiencing the present, and can look to the future. She has lived through the horror and can now tell the world what she saw and experienced. By stepping forward and speaking directly to the audience, while also engaging with the characters in the past, she has command of the entire play. Also, in directly addressing the audience, she becomes more real, more immediate, someone the audience can accept as an individual with an important story to tell.

3. The poem, like the play, emphasizes the importance of remembering. In the case of the poem, it is the remembrance of beauty. Life in the camp was devoid of many of the things that make life worth living, but remembering beauty and being able to create a beautiful poem helps one rise above the ugliness and inhumanity of the camp.

4. Students' music will vary, but should suit the enthusiasm and determination of the words.

5. Students may suggest that without a projector the butterflies could be cut out of paper, painted, or cut from magazines and hung about the stage. Perhaps younger students could dress as butterflies and flutter about.

Creating and Performing

1. Allow the class to vote on the version of the Ludvik the Carpenter song they would like to use in performance. Invite volunteers to perform the version that the class votes for.

2. Ask students to identify each sound by the act, scene, and line(s) on which it occurs. Allow students who have begun a sound log to complete it. Next to each sound effect listed, students can indicate how they would produce the sound.

3. Encourage students to evaluate the monologues they hear by employing the following procedure.
   a) Identify something you admire about the performance.
   b) Make a suggestion for one specific improvement.
   c) Ask a question to clarify anything that puzzles you about the monologue or the performance.

Presenting the Play

For Reading

- Have students work in pairs or small groups to list the five biggest challenges the children faced in Terezin. Invite the groups to compare lists. Then discuss strategies the children of Terezin used to help them maintain the will to live.

- As students read, ask them to think about the differences and similarities between Raja as a child and Raja as an adult. Ask: What does the adult character know that the child does not?

- Encourage the students to make a booklet of quotes from the play that demonstrates the hard-earned wisdom of Terezin prisoners. Ask students to read their quotes aloud.

- Ask students to select a particular poem or speech in the play and read it. Encourage them to keep their readings simple and low key so that the class can focus on the words.

For Performance

- Invite the students to create drawings and paintings that express the thoughts in the play's poems and speeches. Take slides of these artworks and project them as part of the play. You may want to use one or more of these artworks as the basis for a poster advertising the play.

- Allow the students to practice using sound by having them work in small groups to perform a scene complete with sound effects. Remind them to use sound to support the action and mood of the scene; urge them to avoid making the sound effects distracting or intrusive.

- Help students find the music to accompany the Ludvik the Carpenter song. Tape the music for your production. If you cannot find it, there is an abundance of orchestrated music in the public domain that would be suitable to use.

Asides

Visuals
Actual poems and drawings by the children of Terezin are featured in the book *I Never Saw Another Butterfly* (NY: McGraw-Hill, 1964).

Film and Video
Voices of the Children, a film and video containing archival footage from a Nazi propaganda film, includes scenes in which the Terezin children perform the opera *Brundibar*. The opera concerns two children who must defeat the evil Brundibar to get milk for their mother. In the film, three Terezin survivors attend a modern performance of *Brundibar* and recall the significance it had for them as children.
   Black and White Is Full of Colors, a 56-minute film by Tamir

Paul and Alona Abt made in 1996, highlights the discovery of two suitcases full of drawings by the children of Terezin. The film documents the life of Friedl Dicker-Brandeis, a talented Bauhaus artist who lived and worked in Vienna, emigrated to Prague, and was sent to Terezin, where she dedicated herself to teaching the children. Under her guidance, over 5,000 drawings were produced. For information on the film, contact Spertus Institute of Jewish Studies (312) 322-1769.

Internet
www.kks.com/pj/praguetour/ will take you on an internet tour of Terezin and the camp museum there.

Sound Effects
400 Sound Effects, an audio CD available through Madacy Records and Amazon.com, contains sounds from thunder and lighting through diesel engines. Collections of sound effects are also available through Publishers Toolbox on the internet.

Music
The author of this play recommends using the following music in the play:
- Smetana's "Moldau" (the basis of the Czech national anthem)
- The State of Israel national anthem
- Czech folk songs
- Hebrew folk songs

Assessment

I Never Saw Another Butterfly

Reading

Each character in this play has a distinctive voice. Identify the speaker in each of the lines below.

a. Raja	f. Honza
b. Aunt Vera	g. Rabbi
c. Pavel	h. loudspeaker
d. Irena	i. Father
e. Irca	j. Erika

_____ 1. Only one thing is important—that I am a Jew, and that I survived.

_____ 2. I'm not afraid . . . are you?

_____ 3. December 1, 1939. Jewish children excluded from state elementary schools.

_____ 4. I have nothing else to give you but this—what you and all the children have made of Terezin.

_____ 5. As they walk through the Valley of Sorrow, they make it a place of springs.

_____ 6. We will return. You will see, somehow, we will return.

_____ 7. Raja, Raja, where are you going? Come with me to the cinema!

_____ 8. I don't call this living!

_____ 9. Pavel, you are closer to me than parents. I must come with you!

_____ 10. Hush, Raja! Let your father explain. . . . Pavel . . . try to have patience . .

Writing

Write a poem about an aspect of Terezin from the point of view of a child there.

_____

_____

_____

_____

_____

Performance

Perform one of the following activities.

- Choose the monologue that best expresses the theme of the play and perform it for the class.

- Improvise a reunion between Raja and her friend Erika after the war.

- Give a reading of the poem you wrote for the writing activity.

Painted Rain

Plot Summary

Dustin and Teddy, ages 16 and 11, share a room in a foster home. Teddy gets up one day and pretends to be blind. Dustin gets into his wheelchair and begins to paint. When Teddy calls Dustin "my brother," Dustin tells him not to. They argue about the color Dustin uses in his painting. Teddy asks if Dustin would follow him into the pouring rain. Dustin doesn't answer. Barbara, their social worker, tries to convince Teddy to stop pretending to be blind. He leaves. She urges Dustin to use his braces instead of the wheelchair. The two discuss Teddy's upcoming adoption. Teddy returns still feigning blindness, and Barbara tells him this won't stop the adoption. She leaves. The next day Teddy tells Barb that he wants to stay with Dustin. Dustin and Barbara argue about his not trying to walk. After she leaves, Teddy again asks why Dustin wouldn't follow him into the rain. The day before Teddy is to leave, he is crying in his bed. Dustin tells him about the blue of morning light, adding, "Maybe I should paint the sky yellow, like you said." Dustin admits his need for Teddy as well as his fear. Teddy suggests they paint the rain. Dustin tells Teddy that he would follow him into the rain.

The Play as Literature: Mood

- Explain to students that writers use many tools to create and sustain a mood. They can use longer phrases and sentences to create a dreamy, lyrical mood, or short sentences to create a clipped, to-the-point mood. They can use difficult technical words to create a scientific atmosphere or simple words to create an everyday feeling. They can create harmony by having characters speak in similar ways, or they can create tension by having different characters speak differently.

- Write on the chalkboard a neutral line of dialogue. Challenge students to alter the line or add to it to create various moods. Here is an example:

  I saw you arrive at school early yesterday with a big box.

The Play as Theatre: Props

- Students may have difficulty distinguishing between scenery and props. In general, there is an easy way to remember the difference. If it can be carried, it's a prop. If it doesn't move easily, it's scenery. Backdrops and walls are scenery. Tables, chairs, and moveable pieces of furniture are properties. Furniture, lamps, and other props that many characters use are called set props. Personal items such as handkerchiefs, umbrellas, and books are personal props. The reproducible on page 74 can be used to track set and personal props.

- Students are probably well aware of the ways in which people are judged by what they wear, own, and carry. Encourage them to use this awareness to inform their design abilities. Name a series of characters, such as a business person, a rebellious teen, a mother of four, a teacher, and a rock musician. Invite students to name props they might assign to each character.

WARM UP! If you wish, you may increase the interactivity of the game by allowing players to challenge one another's conclusions. Make sure challengers support their ideas by pointing out conflicting details. Challenge the class to come up with a drawing or written description of the "owner" of each object.

Painted Rain

Responding to the Play

1. Most students will agree that Teddy's pretense is based on a need not only to strongly align himself with Dustin but to show Barbara that he is not suitable for adoption. He is also the kind of youngster who would naturally wonder what deafness and blindness might feel like; so he tries them out to experience them for himself.

2. Barbara serves as the adult influence in their lives as well as friend, confidant, supporter, challenger, and voice of reason. She appears at times when the two boys need an issue illuminated or resolved. She serves as a sounding board and a springboard.

3. Students may argue that the dialogue, emotional issues, and relationship between the two characters would, of necessity, be very different if they were girls. Others might argue that the basic theme of the play—the need for love and the fear of losing it—has no gender, and that girls deal with these problems just as boys do.

4. Accept all colors that students can reasonably support using.

5. Essential set properties may include the two beds. Essential personal props may include Dustin's easel, braces, crutches, wheelchair, canvas, paints and tools; Teddy's bag of treasures, sun glasses, orange juice box, and bean bag.

For Further Discussion

1. Why do you think Dustin avoids thinking of Teddy as his brother? *(He may not want to risk pain by becoming close; he may be trying to be sensible.)*

2. What is the difference between being childlike and childish? *(Answers will vary but should include recognition that childlike is a more positive word.)*

3. Why does Dustin say he will add yellow and red to his painting? *(He wants to please Teddy; he recognizes the value of Teddy's perspective.)*

Creating and Performing

1. Allow students to draw their sketches realistically or impressionistically. Students who do not draw well may create collages instead of drawings.

2. Encourage the scene partners to identify the mood of each character and the overall mood of the scene before they begin rehearsal. Invite them to change their evaluation of mood based on what they learn as they work on the scene.

3. Be prepared to offer direction to students in order to focus their portrayals. For example, you may need to remind performers that Teddy acts in a childlike manner. You might also wish to comment on the mood of the play at this initial point.

Presenting the Play

For Reading

- As a way of exploring the relationship between Teddy and Dustin, have students work in groups to write or improvise either the moment at which Teddy and Dustin met or the moment at which they will leave one another. To assist students in developing a plausible scene, remind them to take into account what they already know about the hopes, fears, and habits of each character.

- Teddy and Dustin take turns leading the scenes in this play. In some scenes, Teddy initiates conversation and action, while Dustin responds. In other scenes, the reverse is true. Direct students to annotate their plays in order to identify when Teddy leads the action, and when Dustin leads it.

- Encourage students to work in pairs to read aloud a scene of their choice. Direct them to decide in advance the major event of the scene. Have them identify which character is the protagonist in the scene and which is the antagonist. Encourage students to think about their interpretations of the approaches the protagonist uses in trying to get what he or she wants.

For Performance

- This play can be produced very simply. Aside from the beds and personal props, the only essential element of the play is a large window, which may be set into a flat, drawn on a backdrop, or hung in place with wire. Ideally, the window should have glass or plastic panes, but they are not absolutely necessary to the script.

- Since students acting in this play are likely to be nearly the same age, encourage them to use costumes, movement, and voice to suggest the difference in age between them. Point out that Teddy should wear loose fitting clothing to make him look small. He should wear his hair neatly combed and should communicate in a higher voice than Dustin. Dustin should wear more form-fitting clothing. He should dress and act slightly more "hip," and should be more graceful than Teddy. His voice should be deeper than Teddy's.

- Often, when performers concentrate on mood, they sacrifice pace. Point out that it is more effective to create mood through emotional response rather than extensive pauses.

Asides

Playwright's Corner

Janet Allard was only fifteen years old when she wrote *Painted Rain.* Her work was produced as part of the Young Playwrights Festival of 1989, and has been performed at the Kennedy Center in Washington, D.C., in New York City at Playwrights Horizons, and in many other theatres.

Student playwrights inspired by Allard's work may wish to learn about or submit a play to the Young Playwrights Festival. The yearly festival is sponsored by Young Playwrights, Inc., 321 W. 44th Street #906, New York, NY 10036 (212-307-1140). You may wish to consult local theatre organizations, as well. Many smaller organizations across the country hold similar festivals.

Across the Curriculum: Social Studies

Set pieces and personal props vary greatly, depending on a play's setting. Designers who are familiar with different time periods and places gain a great advantage over designers who do not know history. Encourage interested students to create a stage design reference book for a variety of times and places in history. The reference book may contain drawings, photographs, or magazine pictures glued into place, with labels indicating the time and place to which they belong. Students may choose to feature hand props, individual set pieces, or entire rooms.

Assessment

Painted Rain

Reading

Below are a list of lines spoken by Teddy or Dustin and a list of the words they really mean to say. Match the lines to the underlying meanings.

_____ 1. Maybe everyone else should drink like I do.

_____ 2. You think I can climb a tree with THEM on?

_____ 3. I thought you didn't care about time.

_____ 4. Would you follow me out into the pouring rain?

_____ 5. Barbara's not here to play games with you.

a. Do you care about me?

b. I know you are glad to see Barbara.

c. We are involved in a serious situation here.

d. Just because somebody is different doesn't mean they're bad.

e. I will always be disabled.

Writing

Plays sometimes have epilogues to satisfy the audience's curiosity about the future of the characters. On a separate sheet of paper, write an epilogue for this play, in the form of a letter from Teddy to Dustin and a letter from Dustin to Teddy. Maintain the tone that each character used in the play.

Performance

Choose one of the following activities:

- Perform one of the two letters you wrote for the epilogue.

- With two partners, perform a scene in which Teddy first meets the people who want to adopt him.

- Put yourself in the role of Teddy or Dustin and tell the story of your life.

Nothing But the Truth

Plot Summary

Philip Malloy is a high school student who is anxious to join the track team. He discovers, to his dismay, that the D he is earning in English disqualifies him from track. Philip develops a dislike for his English teacher, Ms. Narwin, who also is his homeroom teacher. One day, Philip decides to hum along with the national anthem in Ms. Narwin's homeroom. Ms. Narwin asks him repeatedly to stop, and he does so. But he hums along the next day, and the day after that. Ms. Narwin sends Philip to the assistant principal, Dr. Palleni, who demands an apology. Philip refuses and is suspended for 2 days. He becomes known as the "patriotic boy who was not allowed to sing the anthem." His parents support his actions, radio shows defend him, and Ms. Narwin ends up being vilified. Philip is blamed for the whole affair, and transfers to another school. There he is invited to sing the national anthem. He confesses that he doesn't know the words to the song.

The Play as Literature: Protagonist/Antagonist

- Explain to students that in Classical Greek and Roman theatre, the protagonist in a play also was its hero—and a force for good. In many plays, however, that is not the case. Some critics believe that the evil Iago is the protagonist of Shakespeare's *Othello* because he is the character who moves the action forward. Othello is the hero, but he is also Iago's chief victim.

- Reinforce the concept that the antagonist in a play may be a person, an inner conflict, or even a force of nature. Invite students to describe or write scenarios in which a protagonist must struggle against a nonhuman antagonist.

- Ask students to name the main characters in dramas they know. Challenge them to identify the protagonist and antagonist in each one.

The Play as Theatre: Creating a Character

- Suggest to students that they can create a fuller, more plausible character if they invent a history for a person they expect to play. Direct students to invent and then share with the class the

  - character's time, place, and circumstances of birth
  - childhood memories
  - best friends/worst enemies
  - events leading up to the conflicts in the play.

- Reassure students that even the best actors occasionally lose their concentration and "fall out of character." As a result, they laugh or become self-conscious. Encourage students to get past such moments by letting the character express the humor or disbelief they experience.

WARM UP!

Encourage the students to develop a character for the monologue by asking the character development questions they have learned. Allow them to "test" their monologues on each other and then revise them. If time permits, allow students to perform their monologues. Ask classmates to describe the character behind each one.

Responding to the Play

1. Answers will vary, depending on students' characterization of Philip. Some students will observe that he fails to take responsibility for his actions from the beginning of the play to the end. Others will argue that the prologue implies that he is starting to ask the right questions.
2. He gets a D in English, hums the national anthem, blames Ms. Narwin, and tells half-truths throughout the course of the play.
3. Students might name as antagonists Ms. Narwin, the media, the school administration, or Philip's own belligerence. A case can be made that Philip is his own worst enemy.
4. Answers will vary. The best possibilities include Caller # 3, who asks for reasoned, intelligent fact finding and Coach Jamison, who advises Philip to be a "team player."
5. Answers will vary but should reflect an understanding of Narwin as a caring, dedicated teacher; Palleni as an administrator caught in the middle; and Stewart as a persistent journalist dedicated to doing her job.

For Further Discussion

1. This play features several turning points, in which one simple decision determines the course of events. What are some of the most decisive turning points? *(Philip's getting a D in English; Philip's decision to hum the national anthem; Ms. Narwin's decision to punish his misbehavior; Philip's refusal to apologize; Dr. Palleni's suspension order; Philip's parents' defense of their son; interference by the media; the superintendent's decision to make Ms. Narwin a scapegoat.)*
2. Do you think it is possible for anyone to tell "nothing but the truth"? Why or why not? *(Answers will vary; encourage students to support their answers with examples.)*

Creating and Performing

1. Remind the students to use language, syntax, and grammar they think Ms. Narwin would use. Encourage them to use Ms. Narwin's letters to her sister in the play as a style resource.
2. Allow students to use either a presentational or representational approach to playing Philip as their classmates see him.
3. To help students expand their understanding of their characters, you might want to allow them to put their characters into improvised scenes. Encourage them to respond in character to circumstances and conflicts outside the scope of the play.

Presenting the Play

For Reading

- Before reading, explain that Philip is the protagonist of the play. That is, he is the character who moves the action forward. Point out that Philip encounters several antagonists over the course of the play. Direct students to list the antagonists Philip encounters and then rank them in order of importance. Hold a discussion in which students can defend their ranking of antagonists.

- Direct the students to write notes on their characterizations of Philip over the course of the play. Also have them characterize Ms. Narwin. Then assign students to work in pairs to read aloud scenes between the two.

- While they read the play, students should try to predict Philip's fate as well as Ms. Narwin's. Write their predictions on the chalkboard and compare them with the actual ending.

- Challenge students, as they read, to identify the principles that motivate Philip, Ms. Narwin, Mr. and Mrs. Malloy, Dr. Doane, Dr. Palleni, Ted Griffen, Jennifer Stewart, and Jake Barlow.

For Performance

- Invite volunteers to form pairs or small groups and choose a scene to read or perform for the class. Encourage preparation by asking students to ask themselves questions about the characters they will read or portray. You might also suggest that they discuss their answers with their acting partners. Allow each group to perform its scene, then ask the class to evaluate the scenes. Which characterizations did they find most likeable? Which were most troubling? Which did they find most plausible? Urge students to give reasons for their responses.

- Explain to students that directors often add to the understanding of a play by using "creative casting." That is, they reverse the gender of characters to provide a new perspective on the issues. Invite a pair of volunteers to read a scene between Philip and Ms. Narwin. Then ask the students how their understanding of the characters and the conflict would change if the student were a girl and the teacher were a man.

- Production notes for the play indicate that scene titles are to be projected on rear projection screens on the stage. Discuss with students alternate ways to display these titles if slides, screens, and projectors are not feasible.

Asides

  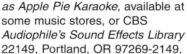

Characterization

There are as many approaches to creating a character as there are actors. Nevertheless, several methods have gained popularity as tools to help actors explore the characters they hope to create. The following texts represent classics in the field:

- *Acting: The First Six Lessons,* by Richard Boleslavsky. NY: Theatre Arts, 1933.
- *An Actor Prepares,* by Constantin Stanislavski. (translated by

Elizabeth R. Hapgood) NY: Theatre Arts, 1936.
- *Audition!* by Michael Shurtleff. NY: Bantam Books, 1978.
- *Respect for Acting,* by Uta Hagen. NY: MacMillan, 1973.

Music

This play calls for the national anthem to be played over a loudspeaker. Versions of the song are available as follows: For the music and lyrics to the song, try the internet site www.usembassy-canada.gov/anthem.htm.

For a CD or tape, try *American as Apple Pie Karaoke,* available at some music stores, or CBS *Audiophile's Sound Effects Library* 22149, Portland, OR 97269-2149.

Sound

To deliver the sound of a crackly school public address system, have a sound effects person fumble with a previously crumpled piece of paper into an offstage microphone.

Assessment

Nothing But the Truth

Reading

Sometimes Philip Malloy tells the **truth,** sometimes he **misrepresents** facts, and sometimes he makes **excuses.** Write **T, M,** or **E** to identify which of the three he is doing in the following lines.

_____ 1. Coach Jamison stopped me in the hall today to say that I should try out for the track team!

_____ 2. It wasn't my fault.

_____ 3. When I was in Mr. Lunser's class, he was like, almost asking me to sing aloud.

_____ 4. Nobody likes her.

_____ 5. I hate her.

_____ 6. I think it's a personal thing with her. She has it in for me.

_____ 7. I mean, if I knew it was a rule—

_____ 8. I'm being patriotic.

_____ 9. Come on. I have to get to class.

_____ 10. I don't know the words.

Writing

Philip has decided to write an apology to Ms. Narwin. Make an outline of the things you should think he should tell her, then, on a separate sheet of paper, write the letter.

_____

_____

_____

_____

_____

_____

_____

_____

Performance

Perform one of the following activities.

- Give a speech defending Philip Malloy.
- Give a speech defending Miss Narwin.
- Give an in-depth news report of the story behind the play.

This Is a Test

Plot Summary

Alan Lefenfeld has stayed up all night NOT studying for the test he is about to take. He worries that Evan, a top student, will get the best grade. A chorus begins passing items around—reenacting a drama exercise stuck in Alan's head. The test begins. Alan knows the Battle of Hastings was fought in 1066, but 1066 is not an answer on his test. Pat taps on his desk. Alan flashes back to his night of procrastination. The chorus continues its rhythmic assault. Chris keeps asking, "How much time do we have left?" The teacher accuses Alan of cheating—failing to notice the students who hold up large signs giving answers. The test questions become more absurd. The chorus becomes accusatory. With only 9 minutes left, Evan walks in. He is given 100 percent without taking the test. The chorus is now drawing comical pictures of Alan. Pat piles bluebooks on his desk. Alan prepares to write an opinion essay, but the question is in Chinese, which the class learned while Alan was at the dentist. Alan's mother wakes him from this nightmare, but when she leaves, Alan is again taking the test. The test is now a personal assault. The teacher announces that this test counts for their entire grade. Alan yells, "This is the end!"

The Play as Literature: Style

Point out to the students that in this play, Stephen Gregg not only creates a conflict between the realistic and the bizarre but periodically blurs the distinction between the two. He does so by blending realistic and bizarre events without any change in staging or language. Encourage students to practice this technique. Direct them to brainstorm narratives, descriptions, or conversations that move seamlessly from the realistic to the bizarre.

Challenge students to write a dialogue between two very different characters simply by using a different style for each character. For example, one character might speak in short, informal phrases, while the other might speak in long, formal, sentences. Invite interested students to present readings of their dialogues.

The Play as Theatre: Timing

Restate for the students that pacing and timing are distinct elements. Pacing refers to the overall speed of a play. Timing refers to the speed at which actors act and respond within the scenes.

To reinforce the importance of timing, lead students in a discussion of everyday activities in which timing is important. Students might be familiar with the importance of timing in throwing, catching, and dribbling a ball; jumping rope; playing hand-clapping games; or braiding hair.

Point out that Gregg's short, quick, active sentences increase the pace of the play. Invite volunteers to experiment with pace by combining sentence and phrases from this play to create longer speeches. Ask them to compare the shorter speeches with the longer ones.

WARM UP! To support students in learning the theatre game "This Is A," establish a slow steady beat by having the entire class tap their desks or chairs with a pen to a single beat. Have the class recite the words of the game to the rhythm you've established. Before you begin allowing students to pass objects around, be sure each object has a one-syllable name.

This Is a Test

Responding to the Play

1. Students will probably write about moments when they felt anxious or paranoid, but their experiences will not be as bizarre as Alan's.
2. Most students will probably say The Voice should sound authoritative, perhaps frightening, even Godlike, and that it should have the resonant, well-modulated, deep tone of an announcer on radio or television.
3. Students' charts should include the observation that Gregg's language is informal, using sentences that are short, crisp, and full of punch. The students, teacher, and chorus are primarily foils for poor, harried Alan. The tone of the play is darkly humorous.
4. Discussions of timing should include an understanding of the play's overall quick pace and the realization that the chorus weaves into the play's action and dialogue.
5. Students should be creative in their calligraphy, using letters that they feel best capture the meaning of the words while also being readable.

For Further Discussion

1. Why do you think Alan's experience is so bizarre? (He hasn't slept; he's had too much coffee; he is extremely anxious about his performance.)
2. How would you portray the teacher in this play? (Possible answers: Portray him as a realistic character saying bizarre things; Portray him as antagonistic and mean-spirited.)
3. What does the chorus represent? (It represents Alan's conscious and subconscious thoughts and emotions.)

Creating and Performing

1. Remind students that they will need to watch their timing in order to speak, listen, and act at the right time.
2. Point out to students that The Voice can say its lines in any number of ways, but Alan must always respond to it with complete belief and seriousness.
3. Direct students to brainstorm or free write about their own fears and anxieties, as well as any they can imagine. Encourage them to make these feelings come to life in their scenes.

Presenting the Play

For Reading

- Direct students, as they read, to make notes about characteristics they perceive in Alan, Lois, Teacher, and Mother. Encourage them to let the text help them make decisions about character. For example, you might point out that Lois's lines are short and direct and that Alan's lines feature many exclamation points. Allow the student to chose one or more characters they would like to play. Then have students work in pairs to read a scene between Alan and one of the other characters.

- In the beginning of this play, Alan is anxious and confused. By the end, he is extremely emotional—at turns hopeful, desperate, and belligerent. To highlight the ways in which Alan changes over the course of the play, perform line readings signifying Alan's state at different moments in the play. Challenge students to identify the portion of the play from which the line is taken.

- Invite students to experiment with pace as they perform some of the teacher's lines. Lead students in a discussion of the ways in which pace can affect the way they portray a character. For example, if they speak the teacher's lines at a quick pace, the character becomes breezy, brusque, or indifferent. If they speak the lines at a slow pace, the character may be seen as bored, maddeningly deliberate, or threatening.

For Performance

- Like the dialogue, the lighting for this play should blur the distinction between fantasy and reality. Blue lights suggesting television can come up at the beginning of the first scene. The lighting should be the same throughout the play, or else it should change with each appearance of Lois, Mother, Chorus, and Voice.

- The author of this play has encouraged performers to experiment with the chorus. It can be more than three people, and it can be performed in a mechanical way or an excessively emotional way, reflecting Alan's panic.

- Use a metronome to simulate the ticking of a clock during the play. You can set it slightly faster at various intervals, as Alan comes to feel that he is running out of time.

- The author notes that every character in this play can be played by either sex. Simply change the names and make substitutions, if necessary, in the section that begins "This is a date."

- You can costume this play simply by having all actors dress in blue jeans and shirts or T-shirts. Teacher can add some emblem of authority, such as a tie or a pointer. Mother can wear a skirt or dress.

- Ideally, Pat's desk should be covered with bluebooks by the end of the play. The daydream sequence offers an opportunity to slip extra bluebooks onto Pat's desk.

Asides

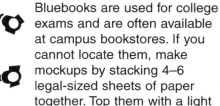

Bluebooks
Bluebooks are used for college exams and are often available at campus bookstores. If you cannot locate them, make mockups by stacking 4–6 legal-sized sheets of paper together. Top them with a light blue sheet of paper. Then fold the stack so that the blue sheet forms a cover. Staple them at the fold.

Other One-Act Plays by Stephen Gregg
The following one-act plays by Stephen Gregg display more of the off-beat humor found in *This Is a Test:*
- *Why Do We Laugh?* Woodstock, IL: Dramatic Publishing Company, 1983.
- *Zero Sum Mind.* Woodstock, IL: Dramatic Publishing Company, 1983.

- *Postponing the Heat Death of the Universe.* Woodstock, IL: Dramatic Publishing Company, 1983.

Assessment

This Is a Test

Reading

Below you will find a list of lines from the play that identify a **realistic** moment or a **fantasy** moment in the play. Write **R** for realistic and **F** for fantasy.

_____ 1. We now resume our regularly scheduled life.

_____ 2. Kai foo len hee!

_____ 3. It's that drama exercise we did yesterday. . . . It's stuck in my head.

_____ 4. Here's the test. I'll tell you what. You don't really have time to take it. Why don't you just look it over and see how you would have done.

_____ 5. This is a kiss.

_____ 6. Athens is false.

_____ 7. Keep in mind that this isn't only a test. This is your midterm.

_____ 8. It's all that caffeine. It makes me nervous.

_____ 9. Which of the following students is most likely to be accepted to Majestica University?

_____ 10. It's too late to study now. You either know it or you don't.

Writing

On a separate sheet of paper, write an essay from Alan's point of view about the time he tried to stay up all night studying.

Performance

Choose one of the following activities.

- Perform a fantasy monologue in which the teacher announces the results of the test.
- Tell the story of This Is a Test from the point of view of Lois.
- Develop an ensemble piece in which several students voice their worries about a test. Allow some of the lines to overlap, and practice the timing before presenting it to the class.

The Frog Prince

Plot Summary

A light-hearted prince is picking flowers for his Fair Patricia when an old peasant woman tells him that he must offer the flowers to her. He refuses and she turns him into a frog, telling him that only a "selfless kiss" will release him from the spell. The prince, now a frog, tries to entice a sweet young milkmaid to kiss him, but she is engaged to another, and will not oblige. The Fair Patricia is quick to marry the prince's cousin, and they take over the kingdom, demanding heavy tribute from the people. The prince's noble servingman sacrifices his life to try to get money to help the impoverished milkmaid.

Years pass. The milkmaid invites the frog prince to join her and her fiancé in the south, but he refuses. She kisses him good-bye and leaves. He once again takes human form, and begins to gather flowers for the dead servingman. The old peasant again demands that he give her the flowers. This time he does not refuse.

The Play as Literature: Dialogue

Explain to students that in a play, dialogue must perform several functions. It must convey information about the setting, tell the story, and allow the audience to learn about the characters. It must also allow the characters to learn about each other.

Ask a volunteer to read aloud the first line of dialogue. Invite students to identify the information contained in that line. Students will discover that the line establishes the forest setting and informs us that it is unfamiliar territory, which suggests that an adventure might occur. It also creates an informal tone, which prepares us for a modern treatment of a fairy tale. Additionally, it shows the prince to be pleasant but unremarkable.

The Play as Theatre: Voice

Point out to students that actors use volume, pitch, speed, and rhythm to communicate their characters' thoughts and emotions. Invite volunteers to describe a situation, indicate the emotion that would accompany it, then speak a few lines communicating that emotion. For example: "I just got a new bike. I am very happy. 'Wow. This is terrific!' " Or: "I'm late for school. I am defensive. 'Gee, Ms. Poe, my alarm didn't go off, and I missed the bus.' "

Explain that actors use emphasis as well as volume, pitch, speed, and rhythm to portray various personality characteristics. For example, a calm, dignified person might speak in soft, low tones, while a nervous person might speak in a high, quick manner. Write on the chalkboard a neutral statement such as the following: *Thank you for the compliment. I didn't expect one from you.* Ask for volunteers to read the line in different ways. Have the class guess the character and circumstances that would prompt each reading given.

WARM UP!
Students who are accustomed to holding their stomach muscles tight may need prompting to relax the stomach muscles and let the diaphragm expand. Tell students the more they use the diaphragm, the more vocal power they will gain. Once students master diaphragmatic breathing, have them add sounds, such as *uhh* or *ahh,* as they exhale.

The Frog Prince

Responding to the Play

1. Students' answers will vary. Some may suggest that the prince will try to reclaim his throne, others that he will live a quiet, ordinary life, perhaps with his friend the milkmaid. Mamet does not suggest that the prince is eager to charge forth and regain his kingdom, and yet it is made apparent that he has learned what is important in life and how to treat others. In other words, he would make a good ruler. However, the prince seems content just enjoying the world around him. He does leave the woods, so he may be going to join the milkmaid, to confront Fair Patricia, or just to start his life anew.

2. Students' choices will vary. One good choice would be the scene where they reveal their respect for one another and their own particular views of the situation they are in.

3. Answers will certainly vary. Some possibilities: Prince, gold or purple, frog, crown, mace, flowers; Peasant woman, gray, white or black, owl or crow, wand, smoke, flowers.

4. Students should be able to come up with many different ways of saying the peasant's line.

5. Students' advertisements should be light-hearted and upbeat, yet convey the underlying emotion of the play.

For Further Discussion

1. In this play, a flower has great value. What kinds of things might the flower symbolize? *(love, nature, beauty, hope, respect, admiration, etc.)*

2. Why does it take so long for the prince to get the milkmaid to kiss him? *(Perhaps because his intentions are not pure when he first asks. When she does kiss him, it is because he has earned her respect.)*

3. Do you think the prince did the right thing in the last scene? Why or why not? *(Most will agree that based on the decision the prince made in the first scene, giving the peasant the flowers was the right choice in the last scene.)*

Creating and Performing

1. Ask students to consider what the prince has learned over the course of the play. Ask for volunteers, male and female, to portray the prince as he explains his philosophy of life.

2. Have students pair up and choose a scene between the prince and the servingman to present. Encourage them to keep in mind how the relationship between the two characters changes throughout the course of the play. After pairs read their scenes, have class members critique the actors' voices, attitudes, and movements.

3. Help students brainstorm what the physical, vocal, and behavioral characteristics of the Fair Patricia might be. Have them use those ideas to compose her speech.

Presenting the Play

For Reading

- Point out to students that each character in this play has certain conversational habits. For example, you might note that the prince tends to run on. He also tends to ask questions without waiting for an answer. Encourage students to identify the speech habits of each character. Discuss with the class what these ways of speaking suggest about each character. Then ask students to read aloud short passages spoken by the characters you have discussed.

- After students have read the first two scenes, offer them the opportunity to write an alternate conversation in which the peasant woman convinces the prince to give her the bouquet or the prince convinces the milkmaid to kiss him. Ask for volunteers to read their new interpretations.

For Performance

- Before reading, encourage students to look at the cast of characters in this play and suggest possible voices for each character, based on his or her stock role.

- On the chalkboard, draw a chart listing each character. Leave room for students to identify vocal characteristics such as length of speeches, speed, number of pauses. After the students have identified the vocal qualities associated with each character, allow them to work in pairs to perform scenes. Encourage students to develop distinctive voices based on the characteristics they found in the play. Remind students that use of a distinctive voice does not preclude naturalness. Point out that the more natural the voice, the more likely they will be able to use it consistently throughout a scene.

Asides

Costuming
Simple objects can convey the idea of a court uniform and allow for easy costume changes. Have the prince wear a green leotard or leggings, a green shirt, a dark belt, and a dark blue cloak or piece of fabric. Attach shiny buttons or medals to a sash and place it over the cloak. When the prince turns into a frog, he can discard the cloak and perhaps add a frog mask.

Vocal Warm-Ups
The following tongue twisters offer students an amusing way to achieve vocal fluidity:

Big blue blob (repeat).
Red leather, yellow leather (repeat).
Sasha suffered a short sharp shock (repeat).

Dialogue Writing
Reveal to students that many writers get ideas for dialogue by listening carefully to snippets of conversation around them in parks, malls, diners, and other public places. Encourage students to keep a journal of interesting comments and remarks they hear at random.

David Mamet on Writing
Most of Mamet's plays include adult material, but he has written two other children's plays, which can be found in the following anthology:

- *Three Children's Plays.* NY: Grove/Atlantic, 1986.

Mamet's books about theatre might also be of interest:

- *A Life in the Theatre.* NY: Grove Press, 1978.
- *On Acting.* NY: Viking Penguin, 1999.
- *On Directing Film.* NY: Viking Penguin, 1992.
- *Three Uses of the Knife.* NY: Grove/Atlantic, 1999.
- *Writing in Restaurants.* NY: Viking Penguin, 1987.

Assessment

The Frog Prince

Reading

Below you will find a list of lines from the play. Match each line to the character who said it.

a. prince   c. peasant woman
b. servingman   d. milkmaid

_____ 1. You know what I want?

_____ 2. They love her as yourself.

_____ 3. Are those flowers for me?

_____ 4. I am touched. I will never forget this moment.

_____ 5. Give them to me.

_____ 6. See here: you have just broken the law.

_____ 7. You say funny things.

_____ 8. Those flowers you must offer me or you will dwell in misery.

_____ 9. Here's what I want you to do.

_____ 10. I am buying this young lady food.

Writing

Write a speech for the prince in which he announces his return to his subjects.

_____

_____

_____

_____

_____

_____

_____

_____

Performance

Perform one of the following activities.

- Give the speech you wrote for the writing activity.

- Demonstrate the way in which the peasant woman casts her spell.

- Perform the scene in which the frog prince tries to get the milkmaid to kiss him. Remember to maintain the physical characteristics of a frog.

The Love of Three Oranges

Plot Summary

Prince Tartaglia is dying and the only cure is laughter. A reward is offered to anyone who can make him laugh. Leandro and Clarice plot to usurp Tartaglia's throne, but Truffaldino, the clown, works to cure the prince. When an old woman tries to feed the prince a potion, Truffaldino stops her and she falls. Tartaglia laughs. The old woman reveals herself to be the evil Morgana and places a curse on the prince. He will love three oranges and will not be cured until he has them. Truffaldino and Tartaglia set off to find the oranges. A magician gives them grease to open a gate, bread to appease a dog that blocks their way, and brooms to give to the Baker's Wife—all to gain access to the three oranges. Each orange contains a princess. The first two die, but the third, Ninetta, lives. The prince falls in love with her. At their wedding, Ninetta is stuck with a pin and turns into a dove. Truffaldino plucks the pin from the dove's head and puts it into Morgana's. Morgana becomes a rat, Ninetta becomes herself, and the wedding commences.

The Play as Literature: Archetypes

Remind students that *commedia dell'arte* features archetypes—stock characters with obvious characteristics. Recurring characters include Capitano, the braggart; Pantalone, an old merchant; and Dottore, a learned but foolish man, as well as young lovers and old masters. Also commonplace are servants, including the witty and acrobatic Harlequin. Each character has well-known traits, but actors can fill in details as they wish.

Commedia actors of old, like many contemporary actors, often specialized in certain kinds of characters. Thus, they became experts at presenting certain archetypes.

Encourage the students to identify archetypes they have come across in literature, drama, film, or everyday life, including the noble statesman, the evil villain, the feckless hero, the mean stepmother, the comic fool, the loyal sidekick, and the damsel in distress. Then have them analyze the personality characteristics and physical attributes they might associate with each archetype.

Stress to the students that archetypes are generalizations. Therefore, they are not true representations of real people. For example, statesmen can be scoundrels and damsels can often handle their own distress quite efficiently. Encourage students to speculate on reasons why a writer or actor might choose to use archetypes—or play against them.

The Play as Theatre: Improvisation

Instruct students that improvisation, like any other approach to acting, has rules and conventions. Early improvisational actors probably played stock characters with predictable lines and movements. They may have even used stock movements to indicate fear, anger, or pleasure. Still, each actor would perform the actions and lines in a different way, and there was always room for new "business," or gags. Today's improvisators often create characters based on their own experiences or observations.

Tell students that the most important word for any improvisational artist is the word *yes*. Explain that to improvise well one must accept the circumstances of a scene and build on them. Invite volunteers to practice this principle by building on the following lines of dialogue:

> Person A: You ate my lunch!
> Person B: Yes, I did, and I ate your hat, too.
> Person A: You ate my hat? Then . . .

WARM UP! Allow students to collaborate in building a simple story line containing a beginning, middle, and end—but caution them against over-scripting their story. Instead, encourage them to decide in advance on each character's motivations and goals. Invite the groups to improvise their scenes for the class, and call "cut" when the scene gets bogged down or confused.

The Love of Three Oranges

Responding to the Play

1. Students' responses will vary, but should include valid reasons as to why they like the character or feel they could perform it well.
2. Ways an actor could convey boredom might include: looking off into space, slumping or showing limp body posture, yawning, frowning, falling asleep, etc.

3.

Leandro	Morgana	Smeraldina
Mean lackey	Nasty witch	Put-upon servant
Plots against prince	Plots against all	Obeys orders
Is finally arrested	Is turned into a rat	Reforms

4. To compare and contrast effectively, students should include elements of either a fairy tale or a film that are similar to this play, as well as aspects that are not.
5. Students' drawings should include Ninetta as a beautiful woman and as a dove and Morgana as a witch and as a rat.

For Further Discussion

1. The characters in this play don't think it is funny that the prince is dying of boredom. Why is it funny for us? *(It plays on a common expression that no one takes to be literal; it places the play in the realm of fantasy.)*
2. What does the audience learn about Morgana in the first act? *(They learn that she is an old witch; that she can be hired to betray anyone, even the prince; that she shows no loyalty to anyone—even those who hire her; that she is egotistical; that she cares only for herself.)*
3. The King calls Truffaldino the hero of the play. What heroic characteristics does Truffaldino display? *(He is loyal, quick-thinking, and determined.)*

Creating and Performing

1. Direct students to write a beginning, middle, and end to their story lines. Suggest that they identify two or more characteristics of their characters before attempting to portray them in an improvisation.
2. Since fairy tales, by definition, contain archetypes, students may adapt any fairy tale, comic or serious, for a *commedia dell'arte* performance.
3. Encourage the students to refer to lists of archetypes they have generated while studying this play.

Presenting the Play

For Reading

- Before students begin reading, introduce the term "suspension of disbelief." Explain that every play requires actors and audience to give up what they know to be true: that they are sitting in a theatre watching performers dress up and say lines. Instead, everyone involved agrees to pretend that the events on stage could happen and, indeed, *are* actually happening. Point out that fantasies such as *The Love of Three Oranges* require audience members to suspend disbelief and accept the magic created on stage.

- After reading the play, have students pick a character and describe his or her physical and emotional traits to the class. Challenge students to identify the character's archetype. At their desks, ask students to practice improvising a short scene, concentrating on the character's voice and facial expressions.

- Have students add a few lines to the end of the play to tell what happens next to the evil Morgana. Ask for volunteers to improvise the dialogue for their endings.

For Performance

- Have students work on developing one of the characters in the play. Suggest that they create a way of standing, a typical gesture, and a word or phrase the character uses often. Students also can describe or draw what the character would be likely to wear. Invite volunteers to demonstrate for the class the character they've developed.

- Have students form small groups. Assign each group a scene from the play. Allow the groups several minutes to improvise their scene. Ask the groups to perform their scenes in the order they appear in the play. (Read aloud unassigned scenes as a bridge to performed scenes.) Encourage successive actors to build on ideas of previous actors playing the same part. Encourage them to adopt physical traits, trademark sayings, and emotional responses for their characters.

Asides

Additional Theatrical Fables

Five more of Carlo Gozzi's theatrical fables are available in *Five Tales for the Theatre,* translated by Albert Bermel and Ted Emery. Chicago: University of Chicago Press, 1989.

Physical Comedy

Commedia dell'arte often employs physical comedy in the form of pratfalls and other exploits. You may want to explain to students that physical comedy is choreographed as carefully as dance. Caution students not to attempt pratfalls or stage combat without adequate training.

Music

Composer Serge Prokofiev adapted *The Love of Three Oranges* into an opera. It has been staged several times since its opening in 1932, and it is available in audio, video, and print editions, including the following:

Audio Recording *The Love of Three Oranges,* by Serge Prokofiev (cassette). Hollywood: EMI, 1983.

Video Recording *The Love of Three Oranges,* by Serge Prokofiev. National Video Corporation, 1982. (French with English subtitles.)

Libretto *The Love of Three Oranges: The Glyndebourne Version,* text by Frank Corsaro, stage and costume designs by Maurice Sendak. NY: Farrar, Strauss & Giroux, 1984.

Juvenile Retelling *The Love of Three Oranges,* retold by John Moreton with an introduction by Mme. Prokofiev. NY: Putnam, 1966.

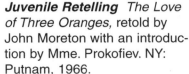

Assessment

The Love of Three Oranges

Reading

Below you will find a list of actions described in the play's scenario. Match the description to the character who carries it out.

a. Prince Tartaglia
b. The King
c. Prime Minster Leandro
d. Truffaldino the Clown
e. Clarice the Niece

f. Morgana the Witch
g. Smeraldina
h. Celio
i. The Baker's Wife
j. Ninetta

_____ 1. She instantly begins to twirl and spin, and before our eyes turns into a large rat.

_____ 2. He departs to seek advice from the witch Morgana to further his cause to seize the throne.

_____ 3. He puts his jacket on backwards. The prince is not amused.

_____ 4. She proposes to be done with the prince here and now.

_____ 5. He can't find the prince.

_____ 6. She brings forth the magic pin and jabs it into Ninetta's head.

_____ 7. He runs to a nearby lake and fills his iron boot with water.

_____ 8. She spins and twirls, turning into a beautiful white dove.

_____ 9. He breaks the hairpin into small pieces so it can never be used again.

_____ 10. She threatens to eat them for supper.

Writing

Write a royal proclamation for the king, offering a reward to anyone who can move the prince to mirth.

_____

_____

_____

_____

Performance

Choose one of the following activities.

- As the king, perform a reading of the royal proclamation you wrote.

- Spin and twirl and turn into either a dove or a rat.

- Develop a comic routine designed to make a bored person laugh. You may use jokes, sight gags, comic routines, or any combination of the three.

Maggie Magalita

Plot Summary

Teenager Maggie lives with her mother, Elena, in New York City. Maggie's *abuela* (grandmother in English), comes to join them in their small flat. Maggie is delighted to see Abuela, but problems develop. Abuela wears black and speaks only Spanish. She calls Maggie by her nickname, Magalita, a name Maggie gave up long ago. Maggie insists that her grandmother learn English, but Abuela resists. Maggie's friend Eric calls and chats with Abuela in spite of their language barrier. When Eric is invited to dinner, Maggie is angry that Abuela prepares a dish made with cow's intestines. Eric enjoys it, but Maggie and Abuela fight. Elena, having had enough bickering, loses her temper. Maggie's fears, sadness, and frustration pour out. Later, Maggie reads Abeula a poem she has written. Abuela understands and tells her in English that it is good. They share a day at the ocean. Abuela dies. Eric and Maggie reminisce about her. Eric asks Maggie if he can call her Magalita.

The Play as Literature: Foreshadowing

Explain to students that foreshadowing amounts to providing clues to the reader about the outcome of a story. Readers who pay attention to foreshadowing clues enter into a sort of dialogue with the writer: They guess what will happen next, and read ahead to see whether they guessed right.

Tell students that they already have experience in picking up the kinds of clues foreshadowing offers. Point out that, in real life, people often provide clues to their future behavior. Encourage students to describe times when they picked up hints from parents or friends about an upcoming trip, surprise party, or other event.

The Play as Theatre: Costumes and Makeup

Encourage students to list some of the things they can tell about someone from looking at their clothes. Then organize their responses into the following categories: Age Group, Social Group, Economic Status, Residence, Personality, Taste. Explain that costume designers work with actors to identify the categories that define each character. Then they choose clothing that expresses how the character fits each category.

Invite interested students to create a character profile for themselves, based on the clothing they are wearing.

Explain to the students that all actors who work in a large space must wear makeup so that the bright lights don't wash out the color in their faces and make them look ghostly. Point out, however, that makeup also supports the costume in defining characters. Reproducibles on pages 70, 71, and 72 can help students develop costume and makeup plans.

WARM UP! Encourage students to invent unconventional or even zany uses for objects in the room. For example, a backpack can become a saddle or a rain hat; an eraser can become a toy vehicle; and a soft pencil case can become an oven mitt.

Responding to the Play

1. Many students will say that the major struggle is between generations. Maggie, in her youth, stubbornness, and impatience, struggles against her grandmother's hesitancy, stubbornness, and fear. Others may say it is a struggle that involves language and cultural differences.

2. Some students will remark on the differences in age, language, cultural values, and habits of the two. Most students will agree that they are alike in their determination, intelligence, loyalty, humor, and willingness to keep trying. Throughout the play each refuses to give in to the other's ideas as to what is appropriate. Each shows her intelligence: Maggie in school and in her writing; Abuela in her adept playing of dominoes and in her shrewd acquisition of language. Both keep trying to connect with and bring humor to the other.

3. Eric's friendliness toward and interest in a person whose language he cannot understand—as well as his ability to communicate with her—foreshadows his willingness to accept and even relish the unusual food he is offered.

4. Accept all poems that show a sensitivity toward and an understanding of *Maggie Magalita.*

For Further Discussion

1. How would you characterize the escalator scene? *(Students may point out elements of comedy, pathos, and cruelty.)*

2. How does Maggie change from the beginning to the end of this play? *(At the beginning she has embraced her American life but turned her back on her Puerto Rican roots. By the end, she has begun to appreciate those roots.)*

3. Abuela had wanted to die in her native land, but instead died in New York City. Do you see that as a tragedy, a worthwhile sacrifice, or an insignificant detail? *(Encourage students to support their opinions with quotes from the play.)*

Creating and Performing

1. To help students focus their gestures and movements, encourage them to choose one character from the scene they select and show movements and gestures only for that character.

2. Encourage students to create a lively sense of diversity by playing each of the four characters differently. For example, one character might be calm while another is energetic; one might be happy while another is sulky.

3. Direct students to make sure the costumes reflect the characters' cultural and social values. Point out that their choices for Elena and Abuela will be rather restricted, but they can use more freedom in their choices for Maggie and Eric.

Presenting the Play

For Reading

- Point out to students that a limited number of readers and audience members will understand all the Spanish in this play. Lead them in a discussion of the advantages and disadvantages of including dialogue that audience members will not understand. (Advantages: emotional content becomes more important than vocabulary; audience members may sympathize with Abuela's disorientation and/or Maggie's desire to communicate in only one language. Disadvantages: some people will understand much less than others; people who don't understand Spanish may be distracted or annoyed by their inability to comprehend some of the dialogue.)

- Challenge students to identify and highlight lines of dialogue that foreshadow Maggie's reconciliation with Abuela. Then have them work in pairs or small groups to read scenes from the play. Direct them to use the foreshadowed lines as moments of drama or change within scenes.

For Performance

- Have students work in groups to identify the age, social group, economic status, residence, personality, and taste of each character in *Maggie Magalita.* You may want to point out that different groups may interpret details about the characters differently, and that there is no one "right" answer. Challenge students to use the information they've gathered here to help them with their costuming plan for each character. Invite them to present their costuming plans to the class.

- Encourage students to think of creative ways to present the play's initial dream sequence. For example, students may want to use a younger child for the scene or costume Maggie to look younger while someone else lies on the couch covered in blankets. Students interested in technical solutions may want to project the dream images on a screen or backdrop or find a way to use video. If time permits, allow students to develop and present their dream sequences.

Asides

Music
The author suggests using a tape composed by Tania León for the play's music. It is available from Southern Music Publishing Company, Inc., 1740 Broadway, New York, NY 10019.

Additional Children's Play by Wendy Kesselman
- *Becca (A musical).* New Orleans, LA: Anchorage Press, 1988.

Additional Multicultural Plays
This play and other multicultural works can be found in the anthology *Around the World in 21 Plays,* edited by Lowell Swortzell. NY: Applause, 1997.

Fiction by Wendy Kesselman
The following storybook by Wendy Kesselman contains Hispanic themes and may be appropriate as core material for improvisations and dramatic adaptations: *Angelita.* NY: Hill and Wang, 1970.

Video
The following video produced for Reading Rainbows (vol. 7), includes a dramatization of Kesselman's juvenile book entitled *Emma,* (NY: Dell, 1993). The video as a whole explores the importance of art in several cultures: *Liang and the Magic Paintbrush.* Lincoln,

NE: GNP, c 1983. Produced by Lancit Media Productions for Great Plains National Instructional Television Library and WNED-TV.

Multicultural Connection
To encourage an understanding of English and Spanish usage, point out to students that idiomatic phrases in one language cannot be translated word for word into another. Allow bilingual students to offer examples of slang expressions that don't translate well literally. Invite interested students to develop an English/Spanish dictionary of idiom.

Assessment

Maggie Magalita

Reading

Below you will find a list of Spanish and English expressions from the play. Match the expressions with the mood or emotion they express.

a. joyful
b. angry
c. worried
d. embarrassed

e. sad
f. loving
g. afraid

_____ 1. You gotta help me, Maggie.

_____ 2. She came, Maggie! She's here.

_____ 3. Abuela. Abuelita. ABUELITA!

_____ 4. It was like a wild thing, that hair of hers. It's so gray now.

_____ 5. You don't understand. My grandmother. She's just—

_____ 6. Para mi?

_____ 7. Shh. Everybody's looking.

_____ 8. Those stairs will be hard for her, won't they, ma?

_____ 9. I don't want her here anymore.

_____ 10. Que linda. Que bonita. Y que grande!

Writing

Write a eulogy by Maggie for Abuela.

_____

_____

_____

_____

_____

_____

_____

Performance

Choose one of the following activities.

• Give the eulogy you wrote for Abuela.

• Use movement, gestures, and sound to describe a zoo animal for someone who doesn't speak English.

• With a partner or partners, pick a favorite scene and present it for the class.

The Drummer and The Big Black Box

Plot Summary

The Drummer, a play told completely in stage directions, is the story of a man who finds two drumsticks in a rubbish heap. He begins tapping the sticks and finds that the sounds of the city act as counterpoint to his rhythms. He continues drumming until he finds his own voice in the sound he creates. The end of the play is the beginning of a new adventure for The Man.

The Big Black Box sits on the stage humming contentedly, then belches. When Arnold comes by, The Box starts a conversation. Arnold is reluctant to talk to a strange box at first, but soon The Box lures him in—figuratively and literally. After taking Arnold's money, hat, pen, watch, wallet, shoes, and coat, The Box finally swallows Arnold. In the end The Big Black Box sits on the stage humming contentedly...then it burps.

The Plays as Literature: Beginning, Middle, End

Ask a volunteer to tell a simple, straightforward story, such as a tall tale or classic legend. Have students identify the beginning, middle, and end. Then invite another student to tell the story of a recent film, such as one of the *Star Wars* movies. Point out that although every story has a beginning, middle, and end, they are not always presented in order.

Explain that authors use many literary devices to create suspense or make a point. Two of the most common are flashbacks and circular structure. Flashbacks provide information leading up to the time of the story. Circular structure helps lend a timelessness to a story by implying that the same things happen over and over again.

Encourage students to tell stories from their own lives using flashbacks or circular structure to add interest.

The Plays as Theatre: Lighting

Point out to students that both *The Drummer* and *The Big Black Box* can be produced with very little stagecraft. Aside from the trash and drumsticks required, *The Drummer* calls only for a tape of distant and intermittent city noises. *The Big Black Box* demands only a large black box. These plays allow performance groups to mount simple, inexpensive productions. They also allow lighting and costume designers freedom in deciding what is appropriate for the play.

Invite students to suggest ways in which lighting can be used to establish or contribute to the mood of each play. For example, lighting in *The Drummer* could be used to suggest a time lapse from dawn to mid-morning. It could also be used as an accompaniment to the drummer's performance. Lighting for *The Big Black Box* can either develop or underplay sinister aspects of the play.

WARM UP!
Ask students to work in pairs. One student holds the flashlight in various configurations while the other sketches the way the face appears in different kinds of light and shadow. Encourage the pairs to identify each flashlight position they try out and characterize it by using descriptive words such as "kooky," "scary," or "gentle."

The Drummer and The Big Black Box

Responding to the Plays

1. *The Big Black Box* begins in an upbeat way, with The Box humming and Arnold moving past. Over the course of the play, however, the plot darkens. *The Drummer,* on the other hand, begins amidst rubbish. As this play progresses, however, a positive energy is created by The Man's rhythmic drumming. In the end, The Man in *The Drummer* is going off to begin a hopeful new life, while The Box's happy humming and contended belch result from eating people.

2. Arnold discovers that he has been outwitted by a box and must pay the supreme price. The Man discovers that with two sticks and determination, he can create music and make a life for himself.

3. Many students may believe that lighting *The Drummer,* with its many props, its interesting character, and its constant rhythm would be the more interesting to light. Others may feel that a sinister box and a gullible human interacting would be the more interesting challenge. Accept all valid reasons.

4. Props for *The Drummer* would certainly include the drumsticks, the garbage can, the chair, bags and boxes, and the cape. Other possibilities are: old radios or TVs, books, newspapers, tin cans, cereal boxes, perhaps a music stand and some sheet music, old toys, and broken crockery.

5. Students' news releases should indicate the name and location of the theater, the date and time of the play, information about the play, who wrote it, and the names of the actors and the director.

For Further Discussion

1. Why do you think Fugard ends his play with the term "the beginning"? *(The character's discovery offers him a new beginning.)*

2. How does *The Big Black Box* change if The Box is played by a woman? If Arnold is played by a woman? If both characters are female? *(Accept all reasonable answers.)*

3. *The Big Black Box* is labeled a comedy, even though Arnold gets devoured. *The Drummer,* on the other hand, has a positive message, even though it is set amidst rubbish. What do these two plays say about comedy and tragedy? *(Life is unpredictable; people need to guard against being exploited; people can make good things come out of bad situations.)*

Creating and Performing

1. Encourage students to use the proscenium or thrust stage outlines from the blackline masters at the end of this teacher's guide. Remind them that the quality of their drawing for this activity is not nearly as important as the concept they want to convey.

2. To help students focus this activity, have them list the qualities Arnold and The Box display before they experiment with voices. Suggest that students create a contrast between Arnold's voice and that of The Box.

3. To add another level of interest to this activity, have the student playing the reporter interview a student playing The Box.

Presenting the Plays

For Reading

- It may be daunting for some students to read an entire page of stage directions. To encourage careful, detailed reading of *The Drummer,* invite students to read the text aloud, as if it were a series of directions for a performer.

- Have students identify the beginning, middle, and end of *The Drummer.* Then challenge them to suggest how the ending might serve as a beginning, as well.

- Ask students to identify the beginning, middle, and end of *The Big Black Box.* Point out that The Box gives us a clue to its intentions as the play opens. Invite students to describe what they think has taken place before the "beginning."

- Have students work in groups to label each of the approaches The Black Box takes to get what it wants. Encourage the groups to demonstrate possible voices and intonations for each approach.

For Performance

- If you direct students to read *The Drummer* aloud, invite volunteers to follow the directions as they are read. Direct the performers to freeze or to maintain their previous action when the readers go over sound cues buried in the script.

- Point out to students that both The Man in *The Drummer* and Arnold in *The Big Black Box* go through a process of change. Direct them to develop a physical style that allows changes in posture, gesture, and movement as the characters change.

- Have students work in groups to develop lighting cues for one of the two plays. Direct them to identify the line on which a lighting effect should occur, describe the lighting change they envision, and indicate the goal of the lighting change. Point out that lighting, like acting, goes through changes during a rehearsal process. Keeping track of their goals for the lighting will help them maintain focus and make sensible changes.

- Invite students to come up with makeup ideas for The Man and for Arnold. The Man's makeup should reflect his economic status; Arnold's makeup can be realistic or vaudevillian.

- In the absence of an appropriate audio tape, city noises can be created by the judicious use of the following sounds: car horns, garbage trucks, slamming doors, shouts of children and adults, ice cream trucks, and vehicle brakes.

Asides

By and About Athol Fugard
Athol Fugard is an accomplished South African playwright whose works have had considerable political influence. His highly charged plays may be inappropriate for many students, but you may want to share with them excerpts from the following works:
- *Notebooks, 1960 to 1977.* NY: Knopf, 1983.
- *Cousins: A Memoir.* NY: Theater Communications Group, 1997.
- *The Captain's Tiger: A Memoir for the Stage.* NY: Oberon Books, 1999.

African Theater
Students who would like to learn more about African theater might want to refer to the following resource:
- *The Theater of Africa: an Introduction* by Lee Warren. Englewood Cliffs, NJ: Prentice Hall, 1975.

Sound Effects
You may want to develop sound effects for this play by cobbling together diverse CDs of traffic sounds, crowd sounds, and the sounds of individual cities. The following CDs contain generic city sounds:
- Volume 12, "City Sounds" (analog), *The BBC Sound Effects Library.* Princeton, NJ: Films for the Humanities, 1983. (Later editions may not include this disc.)
- Volume 1, "Sounds of the City" (analog), *Sound Effects.* Glenview, IL: Ovation Records, 1972.

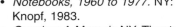
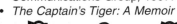

Assessment

The Drummer and The Big Black Box

Reading

Identify the quotes below as part of the **beginning, middle,** or **end** of the play by writing **B, M,** or **E** on the space provided.

_____ 1. Nice day.

_____ 2. *He gets up and empties the trashcan of its contents, replaces the lid and makes a third attempt.*

_____ 3. *He walks over to the pile of rubbish and starts to work his way through it.*

_____ 4. Wouldn't you just like to know? Wouldn't you just!

_____ 5. Oh, don't run off.

_____ 6. *He develops it and in doing so starts to enjoy himself.*

_____ 7. *He has obviously just woken up and yawns from time to time.*

_____ 8. *The lid slams shut, enclosing Arnold in the box.*

_____ 9. . . .am beginning to suspect something.

_____ 10. *He has discovered it is full of drums . . . and he has got drumsticks.*

Writing

Write dialogue for the man as he goes through the rubbish, finds the drumsticks, and realizes what they can do.

_____

_____

_____

_____

_____

_____

Performance

Choose one of the following activities.

- Perform the dialogue you wrote for *The Drummer.*
- Enact a scene from *The Big Black Box.*
- With a partner, improvise a scene in which you try to get something you want. Decide in advance, with your partner, what it is you want.

The Hitch Hiker

Plot Summary

It is the mid-1940s and Ronald Adams is driving from Brooklyn to California. He kisses his mother goodbye and promises to wire as soon as he arrives. As his car hums along the Brooklyn Bridge in the rain he almost hits a thin, nondescript man. In New Jersey, Adams sees that man again; then again in Pennsylvania. Despite the sunny weather, the man has rain on his shoulders. After a night's sleep, Adams sees the man in Ohio. The man calls, "Hall-ooo," and Adams speeds off. Adams is now convinced he will continue to see the man. In Oklahoma, Adams stops to let a train pass—and there is the man. Despite the dry day, he sees rain on the man's shoulders. Adams's car becomes stuck on the train tracks, but he moves it in time. He picks up a girl, who cannot see the man that Adams is now spotting everywhere—and trying to run over. In fear, she runs off. Adams sees the man in Texas and every other mile in New Mexico. Finally Adams calls his mother. He is told that her oldest son, Ronald, was killed on the Brooklyn Bridge.

The Play as Literature: Suspense

Tell students that everyone experiences moments of suspense. As an example, point out that people who stand in line for a roller coaster ride experience excitement tinged with suspense. They wonder whether they will be afraid, whether they will feel ill, and whether the roller coaster will be safe. Their suspense increases as the car of the roller coaster climbs its first incline. They experience some release on their first downhill, but suspense continues to build toward the final incline. The thrill of the final trip downhill is enhanced by the suspense that came before.

Explain that suspense can be thrilling, anxiety-ridden, or even fearful. The suspense of an amusement park ride is thrilling; waiting for test results may produce anxiety; events in a horror movie create fear. Invite volunteers to describe suspenseful situations they've experienced.

The Play as Theatre: The Radio Play

Point out to the students that radio offers unique restrictions and freedoms to the writer, performer, and listener. The lack of visuals forces writers to produce clear, memorable descriptions and sharp dialogue. It forces actors to be especially expressive with their voices. And it challenges listeners to use their imaginations. Yet it allows writers to describe things that are difficult to show. It allows actors to play parts that don't fit their physical type. And it allows listeners to create their own, personalized imagining of events.

To offer students practice in using the visual imagination, play a piece of classical music and challenge students to draw or write a narrative about the story they imagine as they hear the music. Invite volunteers to share their stories and drawings with the class. Point out the variation in interpretations among different students.

WARM UP! To encourage broad participation, have individual students guess one detail each. You might want to have them guess details in the following order: gender, age, occupation, attitude.

The Hitch Hiker

Responding to the Play

1. Most students will say they knew the man was death from the moment Adams saw him on the Pennsylvania Turnpike, because he couldn't get there that quickly and there was rain on his shoulder despite the fact that there had been no rain. Others may say they knew by the time Adams hits the junction in Oklahoma. A few may remain unconvinced until the ending.

2. The fact that Adams continues to see a man who can't possibly be there so quickly is the puzzle he must solve. That the man seems to be seeking him out is frightening. The eerie music and sound effects add to the suspense.

3. Students' choice of music should fit the stage directions indicated as well as the mood at the point in the play.

4. Students may suggest heading out with a tape recorder to acquire screeching tires, humming engines, doors squeaking, etc., or they may believe they could create these sounds verbally, or they may suggest finding them on CDs, videos, or the Internet.

5. Students' posters should suggest the dark and ominious mood of the play.

For Further Discussion

1. How does the dialogue with Mother help establish a mood of suspense? *(Mother communicates anxiety about the trip, about driving, and about strangers on the road, thereby highlighting these elements.)*

2. What was your first intimation that this play contained a mystery? Explain. *(Many of the lines in the first speech develop a sense of mystery. Accept any answer students can defend.)*

3. What do you think is the function of the girl Adams picks up on the road. *(She deepens the mystery because she does not see what he sees; she shows the gulf between normal experience and Adams's experience.)*

Creating and Performing

1. To help students with sound creation, you might want to make available these items: bicycle horns, pots and pans, drumsticks, chalk and blackboard, xylophone, whistle, toy vehicles, wooden board, aluminum foil, wax paper, ceramic bank, toy phone, and coins.

2. Invite volunteers to share their interpretations of the hitch hiker. Encourage students to tell what they like about each interpretation.

3. Students should recognize that the first speech should include tension, but also a forced effort at calmness. The last speech may be more "in the moment," less calm, and more emotional.

Presenting the Play

For Reading

- Explain to students that a playwright can deepen the mystery in a play by providing contrast between the "real" world and the world of the play. Have students work in groups to read dialogue between Adams and the Mechanic, Henry, the Girl, or the Operator and Mrs. Whitney. Direct them to deepen the mystery in those scenes by creating a sharp contrast between the "normal" voice and mannerisms of the minor characters and the anxious, confused voice of Adams.

- Point out that much of this play consists of monologues by Adams. Explain that monologues require variation in tone, mood, volume, and speed to maintain audience interest. Challenge students to mark up a monologue of their choice to indicate the variations they would employ.

- Tell the students that actors who want to audition for professional work often develop and memorize monologues they can perform as samples of their work. Encourage interested students to develop an audition monologue by piecing together the first and last speeches in this play. Direct them to decide whether they want to end the monologue on a note of hope or dread.

For Performance

- Explain to students that radio plays, like stage plays, require the efforts of many crew members in addition to the actors and director. Point out that most radio plays require a sound designer, a sound technician, and a sound crew to carry out effects. If a production is live, the sound crew may stand in front of microphones next to the actors and provide sounds as the play is performed. Encourage students to work in groups to perform a section of this play live, with sound effects. After performing, invite them to discuss the challenges and benefits of working "live."

- Tell students that many radio programs, like many television programs, are prerecorded. That is, the actors record their part, the sound crew records the sounds, and a technician blends them. Challenge interested students to record dialogue and sound effects separately and then blend the recordings into a single program.

Asides

Additional Radio Play by Lucille Fletcher

- *Sorry, Wrong Number,* in *Sorry, Wrong Number and The Hitch Hiker.* NY: Dramatist's Play Service, 1952.

Audio Productions

- *The Hitch Hiker,* starring Orson Welles (one audio cassette, 30 min.). North Hollywood, CA: Center for Cassette Studies, c 1970.
- *The Hitch Hiker* (Tape One), from *The Great Radio Mysteries: Original Broadcasts from Radio's Golden Age.*

New Rochelle, NY: Great American Audio, c 1993.

Video Production

Fletcher's play was adapted for a 1960 episode of *The Twilight Zone.* It was the only *Twilight Zone* story ever adapted from a radio play. The cast included Inger Stevens as a Nan Adams in the role Fletcher had envisioned as Ronald Adams.

Juvenile Radio Plays for Performance

- Adorjan, Carol, and Yuri Rasovsky, WKID: *Easy Radio Plays.* Morton Grove, IL:

Albert Whitman, 1988.

Sound Effects

This play calls for automobile sounds, which can be obtained in numerous CD collections or on the following sound discs, widely available at public libraries:

- Vol. 16, "Cars" (digital), from *BBC Sound Effects Library.* Princeton, NJ: 1991-97. ("Cars and Trucks" are also available on Vol. 9 of the 1983 edition.)
- Vol. 4, "Sounds of the Road" (analog), from *Sound Effects.* Glenview, IL: Ovation Records, 1972.

Assessment

The Hitch Hiker

Reading

Below you will find a list of lines from the play. Identify the lines that produce suspense by writing the letter **S**. Identify those that simply further the plot by writing **P**.

_____ 1. A guy'd be a fool who started out to hitch rides on this road.

_____ 2. You'd think I was still seventeen to hear you talk—

_____ 3. It's all taken place since the death of her oldest son, Ronald.

_____ 4. I am not mad. . . . I feel perfectly well, except that I am running a slight temperature.

_____ 5. He ran off—when I stopped the car.

_____ 6. It's nobody, mother. Just a feller thinks he wants a cup of coffee. Go back into bed.

_____ 7. I knew I would see him again—perhaps at the next turn of the road.

_____ 8. Gee, what a break this is. A swell car, a decent guy, and driving all the way to Amarillo.

_____ 9. No, I didn't see him that time. And personally, Mister, I don't expect never to see him.

_____ 10. He waited for me at every other mile.

Writing

Write the story of this play from the point of view of the hitch hiker.

_____

_____

_____

_____

_____

_____

_____

_____

Performance

Choose one of the following activities.

- Tell the story of this play from the hitch hiker's point of view.

- Perform a scene between Adams and either the Mechanic, Henry, the Girl, or Mrs. Whitney.

- Develop and perform a monologue from the material in this play.

Who's Who in Play Production

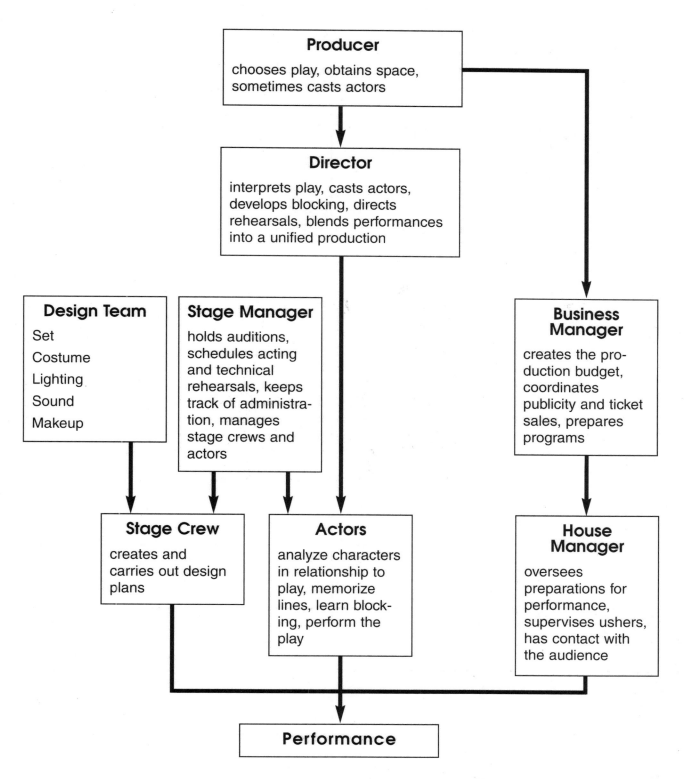

Producer

chooses play, obtains space, sometimes casts actors

Director

interprets play, casts actors, develops blocking, directs rehearsals, blends performances into a unified production

Design Team

Set
Costume
Lighting
Sound
Makeup

Stage Manager

holds auditions, schedules acting and technical rehearsals, keeps track of administration, manages stage crews and actors

Business Manager

creates the production budget, coordinates publicity and ticket sales, prepares programs

Stage Crew

creates and carries out design plans

Actors

analyze characters in relationship to play, memorize lines, learn blocking, perform the play

House Manager

oversees preparations for performance, supervises ushers, has contact with the audience

Performance

Character Map

A character's feelings may change as different events occur in the play. Keep track of how the character feels by completing a chart like the one below.

Play: _____

Character's Name	First Feels	Then Feels	Finally Feels

The Proscenium Stage

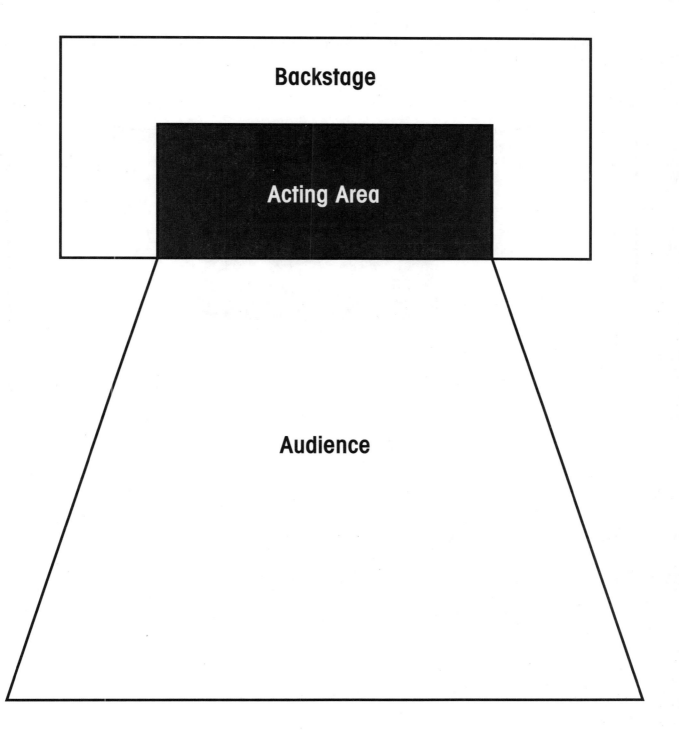

The Thrust Stage

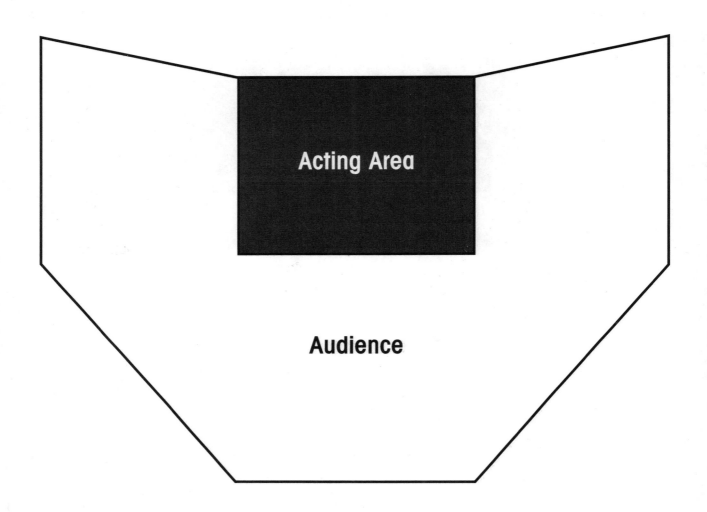

Acting Area

Audience

The Arena Stage

Audience

Acting Area

Audience

Acting Area

Theatre-in-the-Round

(a variation of the arena stage)

Costume Design Worksheet

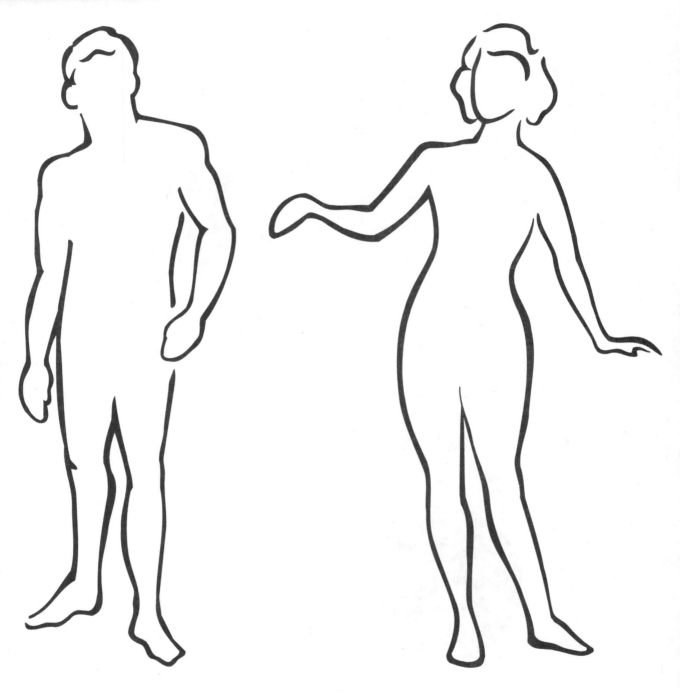

Play: _____

Character: _____

Act/Scene: _____

Costume Plot Worksheet

Play: _____

Costume plot for: _____			
Character	**Act**	**Scene**	**Costume Description/Notes**

Makeup Worksheet

Play:_____ **Actor:**_____

Character:_____

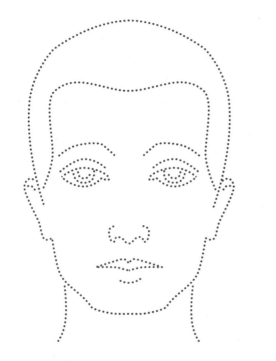 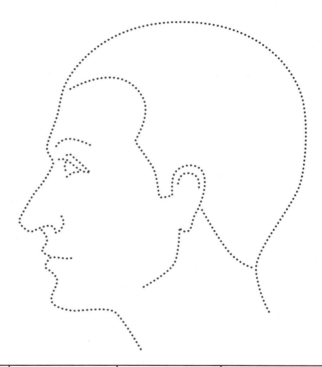

3-Dimensional Makeup	Foundation	Highlights	Eye Makeup	Stippling
	Rouge	Shadows		

Notes	Hands
	Hair

Light or Sound Cue Sheet

Play:_____ Act:_____ Scene:_____

Cue	Script Page #	Description	Execute On	Directions

Set or Prop Planning Worksheet

Play: _____

Act/Scene	Character	Prop	Location	Prop Source

Act/Scene	Backdrop	Set Piece	Location	Set Piece Source

Assessment Answer Key

Arkansaw Bear (page 4)

1. e	4. d, g i	7. a, c
2. h	5. e	
3. d, f, g	6. b	

The Dancers (page 8)

1. ra	4. c	7. r	10. c
2. r	5. ra	8. ra	
3. ra	6. r	9. r	

Novio Boy (page 12)

1. b	4. a	7. c	10. i
2. e	5. f	8. j	
3. d	6. h	9. g	

The Man in a Case (page 16)

1. i	4. i	7. i	10. i
2. f	5. i	8. f	
3. f	6. f	9. i	

Variations on the Death of Trotsky (page 20)

1. year	6. oppressing
2. I'm safe	7. hot-to-trotsky
3. Force must be used	8. time
4. Britannica	9. Smashed, actually
5. THROUGH YOUR SKULL?	10. hope

A Conversation with My Dogs (page 24)

1. d or f	4. d	7. c	10. a
2. a	5. b	8. e	
3. e or d	6. d	9. c	

He Who Says Yes and He Who Says No (page 28)

1. yes	4. no	7. yes	10. yes
2. both	5. no	8. no	
3. yes	6. both	9. no	

I Never Saw Another Butterfly (page 32)

1. a	4. d	7. j	10. b
2. f	5. g	8. c	
3. h	6. i	9. e	

Assessment Answer Key (cont)

Painted Rain (page 36)

1. d	3. b	5. c
2. e	4. a	

Nothing But the Truth (page 40)

1. T	4. M	7. E	10. T
2. E	5. E or T	8. M	
3. M	6. M	9. E	

This Is a Test (page 44)

1. F	4. F	7. R	10. R
2. F	5. F	8. R	
3. R	6. F	9. F	

The Frog Prince (page 48)

1. a	4. d	7. d	10. b
2. b	5. c	8. c	
3. c	6. b	9. a	

The Love of Three Oranges (page 52)

1. f	4. e	7. a	10. i
2. c	5. h	8. j	
3. d	6. g	9. b	

Maggie Magalita (page 56)

1. c	4. f or e	7. d	10. a
2. a	5. d	8. c	
3. g	6. a or d	9. b	

The Drummer/The Big Black Box (page 60)

1. b	4. m	7. b	10. e
2. m	5. b	8. e	
3. b	6. m	9. m	

The Hitch Hiker (page 64)

1. s	4. s	7. s	10. s
2. p	5. s	8. p	
3. s	6. p	9. s	